Blue Apple Switchback

Carrie Highley

Blue Apple Switchback

A Memoir

Carrie Highley

SHE WRITES PRESS

Published 2016
Printed in the United States of America
ISBN: 978-1-63152-037-2 paperback
ISBN: 978-1-63152-038-9 ebook
Library of Congress Control Number: 2015956319

For information, address:
She Writes Press
1563 Solano Ave #546
Berkeley, CA 94707

She Writes Press is a division of SparkPoint Studio, LLC.

Names and identifying characteristics have been changed to protect the privacy of certain individuals.

*It takes many to nurture and love a soul.
This is dedicated to everyone who has held
my hand or pedaled beside me through this
beautiful gift of life. You know who you are,
near and far.*

Sometimes I feel discriminated against, but it does not make me angry. It merely astonishes me. How can anyone deny themselves the pleasure of my company? It is beyond me.

—Zora Neale Hurston

Contents

Prologue

"I declare, Carrie, a whistling woman and a crowing hen are neither fit for God nor man."

I immediately skidded my bike to a stop on the gravel at her feet and slowly petered my whistle out before replying, "I'm not quite sure I understand what that means, Grandma."

"In other words, honey, feminine women don't whistle and hens don't crow, so it's best not to be heard too much as a woman."

Each time I whistled after that, I would quickly bite my lip and finish it up with a defiant sigh. All the while I was thinking, *One day I won't bite my lip anymore.*

Part One: West Virginia

Montani semper liberi.
"Mountaineers are always free."

1
Tides of Change

Never take counsel of your fears.

—Thomas "Stonewall" Jackson, born January 21, 1824,
Clarksburg, West Virginia

My feet seemed to be possessed by some unknown villain from the outside world. They were having their way with me once more, frantically twisting my chair from left to right and back again. The smell of a storm approaching through the cracked office door kept me oblivious to the drops of hot coffee falling in my lap with each nervous squirm. The more I tried to settle my feet down, the more they felt the need to put my body on a jittery merry-go-round ride.

It had been three weeks since Asheville had seen rain, which was causing a hungry brown hue to climb up the surrounding mountains. I was trying my awfullest to read my friend Charlie's e-mail, but the damp fragrance outside was sending me back. All my meditation lessons were not working; I just couldn't stop retracing the rainy day I had met Ryann four years earlier, in Bluefield, West Virginia, at Ira's Coffeehouse. I recalled it had been the first rain in April—the kind that has a distinct smell of washing away the old and bringing in the new.

Now, I grabbed the armrest on my chair and arched my back as I hummed with my lips closed tight, trying to hush these frustrating voices from the past. It was one of those times when you want to forget all the secret places you've been—but I couldn't forget. All I could do was peer outside and let the feelings have their way with me once again. Why was it that year after year I was unable to lock up my rainy-day bouquet and keep it hidden deep inside? More appropriately, I should call it my crying demon, which crept hauntingly from my deepest innards during each looming spring rain, possessing one mission: to torture my heart.

From: Carrie
To: Charlie
Subject: Thank You/Happy 40th

Charlie,

"We are all travelers in the wilderness of this world. And the best we can find in our travels is an honest friend." —Robert Louis Stevenson

I am so very thankful we met on our life journeys. Just think, I never would have run into you if I hadn't picked up the wonderful habit of road biking. I'm glad you're twenty-three years older so I was able to catch up to you and gab your ears off on my first ride in Asheville. If you were my age, I never would have caught you!

Thank you for all you do for the boys and me. It helps in so many ways, and I want you to know how much it is appreciated. Carrie

From: Charlie
To: Carrie
Subject: Thank You/Happy 40th

Carrie,

I know that these are not easy times for you and turning forty is not exactly wonderful. You tend to underestimate your abilities and yourself in general.

I just want to say again that you have movie-star looks and a wonderful, caring personality—with wit, charm, intelligence, and the emotional center to see your way through anything that comes up. I am absolutely sure you will find a soul mate to enjoy the rest of your life with, when you are ready.

I get great pleasure from helping just a little and your boys are really fun. You should be very proud of what you have accomplished; you must have done a wonderful job as a mom in their first years.

Incidentally, I was in the bike shop and noticed that Jeremy has shaved his beard and put some grease on his unruly hair and combed it back. He was the one that asked if you were unattached. Don't forget to bring your bike to the bike shop to have them look at the fork.

It has been a blessing to get to know you and watch you grow during this difficult period.

Take good care of yourself, and don't let the "flusters" bother you too much. We all get them.
Charlie

This e-mail came before Charlie knew the extent of my difficult period or the deep-rooted secret I kept hidden somewhere behind my left rib cage. Each time I allowed my mind the freedom of venturing back, it felt like a piano tune rapping against my sternum, trying to break free and let the world know who I really was.

Charlie knew only that I was going through a very unclear and troublesome divorce that had sent me back to school to pursue a physical therapy assistant degree. His entrance into my life had taught me that people enter our lives to fill a need—that we are absolutely not alone in this world if we only follow with an open heart, and that happiness and sadness do a bit of a waltz with each other throughout our lives. Some choose to make changes; others freeze without ever letting the piano tune escape from their chest.

I had begun to understand that acceptance of change is the only aspiration for true living. Throughout the course of my difficult divorce, my mind, heart, and soul were challenged to their greatest maturity. But I prided myself on saying, "I will never grow up," so of course it was that much more difficult to go through.

When I met Charlie in 2004, I was living in Asheville, North Carolina, with my husband, Sam, and my two sons, Nelson and Quinn, but I had left my heart behind in West Virginia. The moment I first let my heart contemplate abandoning my home and my family had been in 2000, when I was thirty-four. My existence then seemed so simple to me—or maybe I had just come to understand time as a temporary illusion, twisted with reality in every moment.

For a while I was able to find peace of mind, even with multiple moves from city to city while my husband pursued his medical career. Our last move before Asheville was to Bluefield, West Virginia, where my husband started his family-medicine residency. From the outside, my life must have looked like a well-rehearsed orchestra. After all, this was what the world wanted to see: a beautiful woman who effortlessly took care of her doctor husband and their two male offspring without getting lost in the tangled maze. It seemed as though I was trying to achieve perfect harmony in the chaos of everyday living. I was lost, but I was much too busy holding things together to acknowledge it. My mind was teetering on the edge of considering that I may want to walk away from my marriage, but fear always seemed to engulf my hallucinations of a life without an intact family. It didn't matter how many times I told myself I was strong enough and I could leave; I would turn a corner and see the illusion of both my sons' blue eyes full of tears, looking directly into mine, pleading silently, *Don't break this family up . . . please, Mom.* So I would pull up my big-girl panties and settle back into life as I knew it, keeping my crumbling-family thoughts hidden deep inside.

I remember the rainy day in West Virginia when Ryann Garrison walked into Ira's Coffeehouse with intensely radiating confidence. At that very moment my heart began to slip—the damp smell of rain, coffee brewing, chatter and laughter in the background. I was calmly reading my book on the striped red couch in the corner of the room with local art cast along the wall behind me. Sipping on my coffee, paying no mind to anyone else as the intense thunderstorm arrived, taking away my light summer rain.

It's easy to recognize a fellow cyclist from her tan lines, which usually end above their ankles and at the beginning of their wrists. Ryann had those, and she walked with a confidence I knew would translate to stability on her bike when she stood up to push her pedals forward, in hopes of conquering a mountain or playing chase with her fellow cycling buds.

Curiosity got the best of me, so I stood up and made a point of interrupting the transaction that was about to take place. Speaking from across the room as I walked closer to Ruth, one of the sisters who owned the coffee shop, "Do you have any idea where I might find a bike shop in the area?"

"No, but she may know," she answered, pointing at Ryann. "She's always riding a bike."

I looked at both of them with hope in my eyes and replied, "Well, I'm in desperate need of a bike rack for my car."

Ryann quickly took it upon herself to answer. "There's a bike shop about an hour from here, in Blacksburg. I go over there at least twice a week; I could possibly pick up a rack for you."

I became silent for a moment as my thoughts began to stir and my heart fluttered, thinking, as I always did, *How could a stranger offer to do something for me?* Silence was all I could muster up. For as long as I could remember, I had found it impossible to let anyone else help me without an overwhelming feeling of guilt. When I was growing up, my parents always made a point of saying, "Take care of your own business." So, rather than agreeing, I had to give an unsure reply: "Why do you go over to Virginia that often?"

"I own a business over there, and I mountain bike at Pandapas Pond."

Still staggering with hesitation, I said, "Oh . . . I guess in that case, it wouldn't hurt. When are you going again?"

"I'll be going next Tuesday."

"Sounds good to me, but only if you're positive it won't be out of your way." In my mind, I added, *I hope she says it's fine*, because I was experiencing a vast, unknown, queasy feeling that was pulling me to her.

She stuck out her hand as a gesture for an accepting shake and said, "It won't be any trouble. By the way, my name is Ryann Garrison. Who are you? I don't think I've seen you around here before."

I reached for her hand and shook it with a warm firmness. "I'm Carrie Highley. I've just moved here with my husband and two boys." It was a good handshake, one that for a moment put to rest the magnetism that was going on between us. I didn't want to let go but I gradually did.

We exchanged numbers next and that was it—no more teetering on the edge or debating with my heart or mind. Soon after that, back in that little town in West Virginia, I lost the control I thought I had on that rainy day; it fell with the drops and washed away.

2
The Garden

I feel it is healthier to look out at the world through a window than through a mirror, otherwise all you see is yourself and what is behind you.

—Bill Withers, born July 4, 1938, Slab Fork, West Virginia

I could see spring running into the hills of West Virginia as they became green. The mountains there were sharp, resembling the new world that was beginning to haunt my days and dreams at night. The bike-rack encounter was the start of a very stimulating but frightening relationship that included a dangerously high price.

From: Carrie
To: Charlie
Subject: Thanks, as always

Charlie,

Thanks for listening to my tales of woe last night. Your insight was really helpful. You are a wonderful friend. Thanks again for all your help. I cannot begin to tell you how much it means to me. I hope that my small dinners and veggies from my garden repay you a bit.

Carrie

From: Charlie
To: Carrie
Subject: Thanks, as always

Carrie,

Can you please peek at the brand of balsamic vinegar? I think it gave your dressing an extra fabulous flavor.

Anne and I always enjoy your fresh veggies and fresh conversation. Thank you again for dinner.

Charlie

I was tending my makeshift garden when the phone rang. I say "makeshift" because it seemed that every time I had just begun a garden, the following year, month, day, or whenever it occurred to him, my husband would walk in the front door and say, "I'm moving. Are you coming?" Too many times I tried arguing back without success. Plus, I had two small children in tow and a life without a career. So eventually I learned to sigh out, "Where to now?"

This latest move, to Bluefield, West Virginia, would mark move number thirteen. My boys had been in a different school every year since they started attending preschool. With each passing year we would walk in to register at yet another school, office, and county and maybe, if we were really lucky, a new state. Sam had a special bumper sticker on his blue Buick—the boys called it the "comfy-couch car"— that read NOT ALL WHO WANDER ARE LOST. I always felt like we had something of a scarlet letter; the secretaries would look down, scan the boys' files, and see all the different schools, including one year of homeschooling, and more often than not they would look back up at me with a bit of judgment laced with sympathy. Every now and then, if they gave me an extra-long stare, I'd smile with a wink and say, "We're not in the military, and last time I checked we didn't have any drugs on board."

Back to the phone call: while I was in my garden, my cell lit up with Ryann's name. Feeling a bit of tempestuous intrigue meander through my body, I picked up the phone with my sweaty, dirt-covered hand and uttered "hello" at the same time I stumbled over my tools.

Ryann replied instantly: "Hi. It's Ryann. I have your bike rack, and I was wondering if I could drop it off now."

The sunshine in her voice filled my heart. Even if I had been busy, I would have made myself unbusy to spend the afternoon—or even a moment—with her. Still, I was perplexed by the feelings I was having. She was thoroughly stirring me awake while making me absolutely dreamy-headed. How could this be happening to me when I didn't even know her?

With a bit of hesitation in my voice, I answered, "I'm not busy . . . no . . . sure, come on over."

"Where do you live?"

"At 101 College Ave."

"Really? I lived on that road a few years back. Well, I'm out the door and on my way . . . should only take a few minutes."

"Wait . . . when you get here, come around back to the garden. That's where I am. I'm trying to get it cleaned up to plant some spring lettuce."

"Okay," she said, and hung up.

I put the phone back on the grass border encircling the garden and wiped the sweat away from my forehead. Returning to the dry, malnourished soil, I concentrated on the rows. Dust crawled up my legs as my spade tangled with the earth.

I was so focused on what I was going to say that I didn't even hear her car pull up. Ryann was quiet as she came down the steep hill along the worn path between the ivy, and was already close in my space, by my side, before she said, "Hello."

Her abrupt voice startled me; my hand shook and dropped the rocks I was in the process of removing. I turned 180 degrees to look up at her.

"Hey, that sure was fast."

"Well you're only a few short blocks away from me," she answered quickly. "I live on Locust Street, just a little past the elementary school."

Then she bent over slightly and pointed at my forehead. "You have some dirt there."

Trepidation engulfed my heart, then my body, as I awkwardly stumbled to get to my feet and wipe the dirt away. She stepped back and put her hands down beside her thighs. There was a moment of pause and silence as we locked eyes, trying to reach each other's stories—both of which were just too deep and tangled to tell on that spring day in West Virginia.

Finally, I said awkwardly, "Good—I had no idea you were so close."

My "gaydar" was alive and well. I wished I could just touch her in some way to let her know I understood. As I reached for the rack in her hand, our fingers brushed each other's for a moment that seemed to last for an eternity. In that moment I felt a quiet ease between us, born of our knowing we had a common home—one that we had both pushed deep into a closet so we could take care of our families.

"Thanks," I said cheerfully.

"You're welcome. It was no problem."

"Now I'll be able to join you mountain biking in Pandapas."

"I'm going this coming Tuesday; I go every Tuesday around ten. I could swing by and pick you up."

Excitement passed through me again. Without thinking about what the boys or Sam might have going on, I said, "Sure—it would be great to get out and ride! It's been months since I've been on my bike, though, so you may have to wait on me."

She smiled happily and said, "I don't mind waiting. It's a date. I'll be here on Tuesday a little before ten and we can load up the bikes."

As we turned to walk back around to the front of the house, I rolled my whole hand over her shoulder softly and said, "I'm really looking forward to it. I'm sure it's going to be lots of fun."

There are times in life when you can feel the chemistry you have with another person floating in the air, whether it's enchantment or loathing. This was definitely enchantment.

The rest of the day passed in a confused blur, and I prayed for night to come. But when it finally did, I experienced the loathing toward

Sam that had been plaguing me more and more in recent months. Whenever I woke in the night, my mind raced like a hamster on a squeaky wheel: *Should I leave? How could I ever leave? How many people would I hurt if I did leave? Am I willing to come out and lose everything? Where do you find the courage to love someone so intently and with that same heart choose to hurt them? How is it possible to look into their eyes and do this?* All night I went round and round with these thoughts, hoping for happy dreams to take my tormented mind away to a safer place.

3
Pandapas Pond

Diversity doesn't mean black and white only.

—Henry Louis Gates, born September 16, 1950, Keyser, West Virginia

Before my sons were born, I didn't realize how much my love of speed and play would wear off on them. But I should have expected it—after all, I dragged them in a cart behind my bike from the time they were strong enough to hold their heads up. I started out with a single cart for Nelson, then progressed to a double when Quinn came along. I pretty much forced the love of motion on them.

From: Carrie
To: Charlie
Subject: Being a mom!

Charlie,

Oh my goodness, I don't know how much my heart can take. I came home to Nelson and Quinn on my old Razor scooter. They were taking turns riding it down from the top of the mountain. Who knows what the top speed they reached was? I've ridden my bike down from up there, and I get up to forty miles per hour. Quinn came around the corner as I was coming up to pull in the driveway. I tried my best not to have a heart attack.

I hid my scooter. Oh, to be a mom takes patience.
Carrie

From: Charlie
To: Carrie
Subject: Being a mom!

Carrie,
*   And who owned the Razor scooter? I am sure you never went*
too fast on it, just like you never go fast on your mountain bike.
If they did not wear a helmet, you have reason to complain.
Charlie

Tuesday arrived quickly, and Ryann pulled into the gravel drive-way with her Subaru at 9:53 a.m. I heard the jangle of gravel under the tires as I replaced the top on my CamelBak. I put my helmet under my arm, grabbed the rest of my gear, and ran to the front door. Stumbling with my nervous energy, I tripped over the front threshold and dropped my helmet and gloves on the front porch. Amid this blundering behavior, all I could think was, *I can't wait to get into the car with that West Virginia redhead.*

As I was collecting myself and my items, Ryann rolled down her window and yelled, "Walk much?"

All I could think to do was look up and smile as big as my mouth would let me, giggle a little, and hope this would ease the embarrassment of yet another awkward moment in front of her.

Ryann jumped out and helped me put my bike on her rack and we strapped it down together. I put my shoes, change of clothing, and CamelBak in the backseat, and then we got in the car, backed out of the driveway, and headed toward 460 East and Pandapas Pond.

A restless silence took over after the first few miles of the trip as we sat side by side. Finally, deciding to break the ice, I asked, "How long have you lived in Bluefield?"

"All my life," she replied. "Born and raised here."

"Wow, you don't see that very often, someone living as an adult in their hometown—or maybe it's just I've moved so much and haven't been back to my hometown in years. All I wanted to do was run from

Greensboro and never look back. I guess I just wanted to see what the rest of the world had to offer. The South is kinda tight and stuck in its ways."

Ryann turned and glanced at me pointedly for a moment. I looked at her but quickly turned away from the awkwardness to look down at my feet. I was hoping she wasn't feeling my desire, but just in case, I decided to distract her. "What about your family? Any brothers or sisters?" I asked.

"I had two sisters, but they both died at a young age."

"Oh, really?" I replied, my voice full of sympathy. "How?"

"One committed suicide, and the other died at the wheel of a drunk driver."

What do you say to someone who has suffered something of this magnitude? The usual human reply: "Ummm . . . I'm sorry"? In the never-ending abyss of words, is there one that can top "sorry" or make it all better? No—especially not from me, someone without the personal experience that might have helped me feel the real empathy I needed at that moment. So I offered the typical response: "I'm sorry."

"It's okay," she said, with a flat but sure affect, as if she had heard that reply a million times before. Her demeanor didn't change; I guessed she had eventually learned to live with loss and thought there wasn't any use fussing over it.

"What about you?" she asked. "Do you have any brothers or sisters?"

"Yes, I have two sisters and one brother, all alive and well."

"So do any of them live back home in Greensboro?"

"No, we're pretty much spread all over the East Coast. One in Key West, one in DC, and the other Atlanta."

"That sure is a lot of distance between you all. I guess you don't get to see each other too often." She sounded surprised.

I looked out the window and replied with a somber, flat "no." My siblings and I had been close as kids, but now the abandoned emotions between us were almost as wide as the miles separating us. Busy grown-up lives have a way of doing that—teaching you to buckle down and be responsible in the here and now, leaving little time to pay attention to family far away. Also, the distance between us helped me keep hiding the secret I didn't know how to reveal.

Turning back to look at Ryann, I smiled—I was tickled to be in the car with her. My thoughts and dreams for the last week had been centered on this moment; now that it had arrived, I was like a kid in a toy store. We were soon so caught up in conversation that I didn't feel the hour slip away, and before I knew it we were pulling into the large gravel parking lot at Pandapas.

We got out of the car and quickly unloaded our bikes. There were only a few other cars in the lot, which meant we would have the trails all to ourselves. We could jump and play without worries of running head-on into someone around a switchback. I knew it must be a whole other story on the weekends, when the lot would be full and the trails congested with people.

I wasn't sure which one of us was more excited, but the second we had our bikes off the car, we both were struggling as fast as we could to get our CamelBaks and shoes on. After we were dressed I offered to pump the tires up, making sure to put in the right amount of pressure to hopefully avoid a pinch flat over the rocks. Finally dressed and ready, we were on the trails by a little after eleven.

As we took off on the first downhill, I looked at Ryann's extra-muscular thighs, which resembled a thoroughbred stallion's legs, and I gulped, overcome with the sinking feeling I was going to have trouble keeping up. She naturally took the lead on the single tracks. I would soon come to learn she was a born leader at work and in her social life.

I have a competitive nature, so it hurt my ego to have to chase Ryann along the rocky paths. When I called out to make sure she knew I was right behind her, each word required its own labored breath: "I'm . . . coming . . . don't . . . you . . . worry . . . about . . . me . . . I'll . . . catch . . . up."

I was able to keep up on the downhills, but when we got to the uphills it was a different story. Ryann was an excellent climber: on the first ascent, she nimbly climbed over the rocks and up and around the bend in the trail, and before I knew it she was out of my sight. I huffed and puffed, sucking all the air I could squeeze into my lungs as I chased her. I was able to play catch-up on the downhill because of my lack of fear, but she left me behind again on the next uphill.

We were about an hour into our ride when I came around a bend in the trail after some pines and found Ryann off her bike, inspecting her back tire. I skidded in the gravel a bit, before stopping abruptly beside her, just to put on a little show. I wanted her to know that I had this whole biking thing down.

"I have a flat," she said with a tinge of anger in her voice.

"I'm kind of glad you do. It will give me time to catch my lungs and legs up to you."

She turned up the right side of her mouth, then the left, and let out a little championship giggle through her slightly opened lips. Her eyes had an intriguing twinkle and just enough crow's-feet around them to tell she had an interesting story set behind them. I would try my best not to love her giggle, red hair, freckles, and amazingly strong appetite for life, but I already suspected my might would not be sufficient. There are people in life who radiate spunky positive energy without effort—natural human magnets. Ryann was one of those special people, and in that moment, I knew that biking with her would change me and the course of my life forever.

Realizing that we would be there for a few minutes, I let out a sigh of relief—and anticipation. Not only would I benefit from the much-needed rest while Ryann changed her tire, but the break was the perfect chance to spend more time with her, witnessed only by the eyes and ears of nature. In one swift motion, I swung my right foot over my saddle and landed on the ground. With a quick jump in the air and delight in my voice, I said, "Let's get that tire changed."

After changing the tire, we rode for another hour through creeks, rhododendron thickets, muddy, rooty paths, and gravel fire roads. I was grinding in high gear on all the flats and on downhills. On the climbs I was in my granny gear, spinning as fast as I could in hopes I would gain on Ryann. My muscles were working overtime, beyond their strength and ability; I could feel my legs quivering with fatigue on the downhill sections where I was able to coast a bit. But there was a fire inside me keeping me going. I wasn't sure where it was coming from, but I was pretty confident that Ryann was the warmth and oxygen I was chasing to sustain it.

At the end of the ride, we were covered with specks of mud from head to toe, and my socks and shoes were soaked. We had both had the foresight to bring a change of clothes, and we took turns going into the woods to change.

"You go first; I'm going to clean my face with my towel before I change," I said, digging around in the backseat for my things.

She made her way down the short bank into the woods before disappearing from view and yelled over her shoulder, "Would you like to go into Blacksburg to eat at Gillie's?"

I had been to Gillie's—a really yummy, eclectic vegetarian restaurant in Blacksburg, Virginia—many times with the boys and Sam, and the thought was appealing. But, looking at my watch, I realized I shouldn't go. "If I go into town now, we may not get back in time for me to pick the boys up from school," I hollered back.

"I could call my sitter, Chelsea," Ryann replied from behind the shelter of a few rhododendron bushes. "She can get Alex and the boys at school and take them to my house until we get home." Ryann's son, Alex, was in the same class as my younger son, Quinn, and Nelson was two grades ahead of them. Ryann's husband, Jim, worked long shifts as a public defender and was rarely available to help with childcare, so she relied heavily on Chelsea.

I agreed without hesitation, though inside I was having a cowardly sort of guilt for not overcoming my desire and saying no. It would be the first time I was not at school for the boys. But I felt like being selfish.

"I'll call Sam and have him pick them up from your house after he gets off work. They can go have dinner together."

"Okay, sounds good. We'll get changed and head that way."

—

We had a wonderful, stimulating conversation at Gillie's—unlike what my conversations with Sam had become. The history he and I had together taught us to understand our encrypted language of together-ness—the language of Sam and Carrie. We both accepted how we took each other for granted because the thought of leaving each other cre-ated too much agony. Over the course of our twelve-year relationship, we had developed a pattern of pseudo togetherness that disguised how little connection we actually shared anymore. We maintained the charade because the alternative—splitting up—was too scary and agonizing for either of us to consider.

I got home just before dark, when the stars were peeking through the night air and the crickets had just begun to play their tune. My body was spanked and beaten; I barely had enough strength to help Ryann get my bike and equipment onto the front porch.

I turned to look at her as she was closing her car door. "I'm tired," I said, rolling my shoulders.

"But it's a good tired," she yelled out the window, already backing out of the driveway. "Let's plan on it again next Tuesday."

"For sure, I can't wait!" I said before turning to the front door, where I paused for a moment. I could hear giddy little-boy laughter mixed with shuffling seeping from under the door. It was the familiar sound of Sam, Nelson, and Quinn wrestling together on the floor in the den.

I looked back to watch Ryann's lights fade into the dusk, and a feel-ing of fullness tangled with emptiness captured my heart.

4
Roadie

None who have always been free can understand the terrible, fascinating power of the hope of freedom to those who are not free.

—Pearl S. Buck, born June 26, 1892, Hillsboro, West Virginia

From: *Carrie*
To: *Charlie*
Subject: *Ride Saturday*

Charlie,

Thanks for agreeing to pick Quinn up from school for me tomorrow. I think he enjoys spending time with you.

Are you planning on doing the Jack's Creek ride on Saturday? I hear it is a ride not to be missed. This girl is in need of some pedaling!

Carrie

From: *Charlie*
To: *Carrie*
Subject: *Ride Saturday*

Carrie,

If I've told you once I know I've told you many times I don't mind helping with Quinn and Nelson. I am very blessed to

have a wonderful life. I am especially blessed to be able to give a little nudge to help others achieve their dreams.

I'm definitely doing the Jack's Creek ride. It starts at 10 in the morning, if you come to my house at about 8:45 in the morning we can ride together up to the start. There are no bathrooms at the start, so we will need to stop on the way. The colors should be awesome. Temperatures at the start should be above sixty degrees and high of seventy-six is the forecast with twenty percent chance of rain and low winds. It should be a fabulous day for riding.
Charlie

Jack's Creek, North Carolina could switch places with Clover Hollow, which is just outside the town of Narrows in Giles County, Virginia. Both have alluring yellow meadows and creeks that meander throughout the rides. The sun rises and sets in Clover Hollow a few minutes before Jack's Creek, but you would never know it unless you were in both places at the same time—an impossibility, since they are approximately 210 miles apart. The roads in both of these places are also full of switchbacks, and you can't see clearly around most of the curves. You have to learn to trust and have faith that it will be okay to move forward.

Clover Hollow was my favorite place to ride road bikes with Ryann. Each time we headed East on 460 to Pandapas for our mountain bike rides, Ryann would point to the left, give a nod toward Narrows, and say, "You're going to have to try a road bike one of these days."

At this I always frowned and wrinkled my nose. "I don't think I have it in me to hang up my mountain-biking shoes," I would say. "I don't take myself for a roadie." Riding on smooth pavement—only seeing the creeks and woods from a distance, and having to try to avoid cars at the same time—just didn't sound enticing to me.

"But it's different," Ryann said, "and a different I'm sure you would really enjoy."

And that's how it happened: after weeks of this back-and-forth debate, Ryann talked me into going over to the new bike shop in Princeton, West Virginia, to test-ride a road bike.

—

We went to the bike shop early one afternoon, before the kids were out of school. I was all thumbs and two left feet when I first got on the bike. The gear controls on the bike were on the brakes, and you had to turn them sideways while making sure you didn't squeeze . . . *because squeezing would stop you.* Not a good combination for someone who constantly trips over her own toes and often walks around with skinned knees.

There were two gears on each brake, one to shift up and one to shift down, with each side controlling either the front chain ring or the rear cassette. You had to slide one control and click the other, all the while keeping in mind that each movement up or down would make the gears easier or harder. As if this wasn't enough to worry me, there was also the fact that my feet would be clipped onto the bike pedals—a thought that sent quick, cool shivers down my spine. I was going to become one with the bike. I hadn't attempted to swim in those waters on my mountain bike yet, so to do it while pedaling on tires as thin and slick as a baby garden snake was nerve-racking.

I rode around for about thirty minutes in the parking lot and down a side street. Ryann stood watching with hopeful anticipation in her eyes as I twisted in and out of parked cars. After playing with the gears and brakes and stopping too quickly a couple of times, my heart was hooked. I was ready to buy a road bike.

I rode up beside Ryann and said, "I love the fastness of this!"

"I knew you would—it's great isn't it? I kept trying to tell you."

I couldn't contain my enthusiasm. "Yes it's wonderful! I can't imagine what it will be like on the open road." Looking down, I sighed. "I do feel a little like a goober on it, though . . . trying to learn how these gears and levers work without pushing the brakes."

"With just a little time and practice, you won't even have to think about it, I promise," she said encouragingly.

———

It was a silent ride home to Bluefield. I was stuck inside my head, busy conjuring up how to persuade Sam that buying a road bike for me was a good idea.

Ryann dropped me at the house just in time to get on my foot scooter and head over to school to pick up the boys. She was picking Alex up too, but first made a quick run to her office two blocks away.

I scooted up to the side door at the school and, after pushing my scooter under the prickly holly bushes where we had hidden the boys' scooters early that morning, entered quickly, hoping I'd beaten Ryann there. Once inside, I spotted her standing with her back to the gray lockers just beyond the doors.

We caught each other's eyes and I smiled but looked away, afraid of showing her too much attention. Our emotions were beginning to intertwine with one another's, and I feared my fondness of her was becoming visible.

Feeling self-conscious about the quick glance, I halfway waved and said, "Hey."

She wasn't even looking my way by then; she had already begun to speak with another mom. But instead of waiting until they were done, in my clumsy way, I stepped out from the lockers and waved again, this time with an exaggerated wave and a really loud, "Hey!"

She looked in my direction and acknowledged me with a wave, but kept talking to the other mom.

The kids were beginning to trickle out onto the maroon linoleum that looked to be a remnant from the fifties, moving like a stream between the parents and sitters who were leaning on either side of the hall. Some of the kids were running quickly, as if to escape, while others were walking at a leisurely pace, putting books in their bags as they went. Back in elementary school I was one of the kids running as fast as I could to freedom; I was a bit of a misfit growing up, a square peg that had a hard time fitting into this round world. I came to school each day trying to hide the dirt covering me—not literally, but it was there, and in my mind it was very visible. When you're a kid, image is everything. I stuck with the crazy kids who accepted me blisters and all. I promised myself I would never let this happen to Nelson and Quinn, but it was inevitable with all the moving we did. Like me, they had learned to make friends with the ostracized kids so they wouldn't be alone in their new environment.

I could see my sons now, their feet slapping stiffly on the linoleum as they ran down the hall, looking to me with big smiles on their faces.

I was delighted to see them. "How was your day?" I asked enthusiastically.

"It was okay, but let's go," Nelson said, already pulling my arm toward the door.

"Good!" Quinn exclaimed, reaching for my other hand and jumping high in the air.

I looked over my shoulder as the boys led me through the doors. Ryann and Alex had already locked arms; they were caught up in their own after-school greetings. They looked so happy with one another. She was so convincing in her act, I never could have guessed how much she was suppressing her unhappiness, deep down in a place only she could visit.

When we got outside, I tried to stall a little bit by pulling our scooters out of the bushes nice and slow, hoping to catch one more glimpse of Ryann before we left. That steady, uncontrollable desire to spend time with her was nudging at my heart again.

But the boys were both ready to go. "Hurry up, Mom!" they yelled at the same time.

As we were all getting on our scooters to skate away, Ryann finally came down the steps. "Biking next Tuesday?" she called out, quick and loud.

My body quivered a little bit and I couldn't answer at first, but a few seconds later I caught my reply and blurted it out: "Sure, give me a call this weekend." What I was really thinking and wanting to say was,

"Can we ride tomorrow?"—but the courage wasn't there, so I kept that thought to myself.

We scooted the six blocks home on the sidewalk, me in front and the boys trailing closely behind. I'm sure they were thinking of their swing set at home as I was thinking of Ryann Garrison back on the steps at the school. I made a point of leading them the long way home.

Every day we put a rhythm together that went *bumpity-bump* over the concrete squares all the way home, and we sang songs like "Zip-a-Dee-Doo-Dah" and "Shady Grove" as we weaved in and out of the broken parts of sidewalk along the way. We were completely out of tune with one another while I whistled and the boys sang, but we all loved this afternoon ritual. Because I had a secret I was unwilling to reveal, I hoped that my boys would see me as an unconventional mother, realize that it was okay to be different, and find the bravery to stand alone in their own lives.

——

At home, we tossed our scooters inside the house, across the wood floors, and I went straight out to my garden, while the boys scrambled down the hill to their swing set. They became caught up in a contest to see who could make the highest arc in the air followed by jumping out far onto the grass. Their little-boy giggles made me as content as the buzzing honeybees pollinating the pink cosmos beside me. I got caught up in hoeing and weeding the dusty, dry dirt for an hour or so, envisioning my next ride with Ryann all the while.

We played hard at our activities for about an hour, and then I went in the house to cook dinner while the boys stayed outside and challenged each other longer into the evening. As I was getting our meal onto plates, Sam walked silently into the kitchen, came straight over to me, and delicately put one hand on my shoulder and his other hand on my waist, just to the front of my pelvis, to strategically pull me back into him. I could feel the outline of his body melting into mine. He proceeded to softly kiss the nape of my neck.

I pulled slightly away, pushing his hand and my stomach into the sink. Realizing I was trapped, I avoided his kiss with conversation, breaking free of his grip by turning around to look up at him.

"How was your day?" I asked him with a bit of irritation in my voice. Recognizing that this would not help me acquire money for the purchase of a road bike, I paused—and then I thought to myself, *What is making me stoop this low and be so selfish?* I had been so centered on how I could spend more time with Ryann that I'd been ignoring Sam entirely. Feeling guilty, I quickly reached with both of my hands and pulled him back to me and into my chest, tilting my head back just enough to receive a small kiss.

"Could you help me get the plates ready? The boys have been outside since we got home from school."

"Sure, that's what I was trying to do," he replied, snatching a plate up and pinching up a serving of salad roughly before dropping it onto the plate. There was a sharp echo from the contact of the tongs with the plate; it sounded like fear and anger.

I put my hand on top of his. "What were you expecting? You startled me, and I needed a minute to catch my composure. I'm sorry."

Sam answered with his usual prideful, deep tone, "I try to be nice and show my love for you and this is what I get. You're pulling away and I can feel it."

He removed his hand from under mine and turned away from me with the plate to make his way over to the stove. He bitterly knocked his shoulder against mine as he moved by me. Fear from both of us was filling up the room; I knew it was time for me to be quiet. I went out on the porch to call the boys in to eat.

I stood at the railing with my arms folded and breathed deeply to take in the cool air. I needed to savor the innocent sounds of the boys and forget the meanness I was feeling toward Sam. Looking down from the railing at the boys, who were still laughing and scampering around, I yelled, "Hey guys, it's time to eat dinner."

Quinn looked up and yelled back, "Aww . . . can't we have two more jumping contests?"

"I suppose two more is okay, but come up and wash your hands as soon as you're done. By the way, your dad is here."

"Yeah!" they both yelled back at the same time with happy excitement.

I turned back to the kitchen and walked right back into the thick emotions that were filling the air like a hot steam room. Dinner would be a long journey to get through if I didn't patch things up with Sam.

All the dishes were full and on the table, and he was working on filling the glasses with water.

I came up beside him and said with what I hoped was an inviting voice, "You didn't tell me how your day was?"

The air cleared a little with my invitation to talk, and he replied, "It was fast and I'm really tired; I think I saw twenty patients today."

The boys ran into the kitchen and skidded across the white tile floor right into Sam. Quinn hugged his legs as Nelson grabbed him tight around the waist. Looking at the three of them, I could feel in my heart a burning gratitude that said, *Thank you for making it possible for me to be with them and take care of them every day.* Sam must have felt the warmth, or seen it in my eyes, because calmness moved into the room along with the boys.

I stopped filling the fourth glass with ice so I didn't have to speak over the grind and growl of the icemaker and said again, this time with force, "I'm sorry." I wanted him to know I really meant it. He was working hard to accomplish his goal of finishing his family medicine residency while I got to be home and enjoy my time with the boys.

"Its okay," he said, struggling to stand up as both the boys tugged on him at the same time.

The steam dissipated as we all moved into the dining room together to eat, and for most of the meal I forgot about Ryann and my unrelenting desire for a road bike. The anxiety in the air disappeared long enough for the boys to interrupt one another with their stories about their day at school. But as Sam listened to them very intently, my mind drifted back to Ryann once again. Something was wrong—she just kept running through my brain without warning.

When we'd finished our meals, a silent streak took over the table. I thought the silence was the perfect opportunity to mention my earlier bike ride with Ryann, so I spit it out, almost stumbling over my own words.

"I went with Ryann today to test-ride a road bike."

"Really." Sam looked up for a second, then back down as he moved his fork across the plate, making a clean, scratching sound.

"Yep, it was so much more fun than I imagined it would be. I was awkward on it at first, but I started to get the hang of it after about thirty minutes of riding. It was exhilarating, fast fun."

He dropped the fork on the plate and let out a bit of a grunting sound, then looked directly at me and said, "Well, how are you going to find time to do that in addition to mountain biking?"

His reply startled me a little, and I clasped my hands together under the table and wrenched them back and forth for fear he could see Ryann running around in my brain. When you live with someone for many years, you create a sort of ebb and flow with one another, and you can feel when the pattern is interrupted. I was shaking up the balance we had created, and Sam was becoming aware of it.

The boys got up at the same time, grabbed their plates, and quickly scooted to the kitchen sink, then back by us and up to their room. They knew it was Mom-and-Dad-conversation time.

My desire spoke over my fear at that moment. I looked right at Sam and without hesitation I asked, "Do you think I could buy a road bike?"

5
Crash

Coalwood's miners proudly dug the finest bituminous coal in the world, all of it shipped to the steel mills of Ohio and Pennsylvania.

—*The Coalwood Way: A Memoir*, by Homer Hickam,
born February 19, 1943, Coalwood, West Virginia

In all my years of mountain biking, I had learned about cold weather riding and layering, but it was a different beast on a road bike. I got really hot and sweaty on the extended climbs, but those were followed by long, chilly downhills. If I had the wrong layers—too many or too cheap—my sweaty clothes froze to my skin. In the woods I had the protection of the trees, along with short stops, to catch a break from the icy air, but road riding in the open air at high speeds gave me a frigid education on new types of materials for staying warm.

From: Carrie
To: Charlie
Subject: Postal

Charlie,
I need some exercise before I go postal. Tried running again and my knees started hurting, so I guess I will get some bicep exercise with "whine" tonight.

I wish the weather would improve so I could just get on my bike.
Carrie

From: *Charlie*
To: *Carrie*
Subject: *Going Postal*

Carrie,

What is going postal? You can tell I'm old.

The Grove Park Inn has spin class at 8:00 a.m. on Saturday if you really want to get on a bike. But you would have to get up early. No sleeping in.

The other option is to ride at 10:00 a.m. until noon, when it is supposed to start raining, but it will be thirty-two degrees.

Have you considered walking fast up your mountain rather than jogging? You can get almost as much exercise, especially considering how steep your hill is.

The offer is still available to lend you my trainer.

Looking ahead at the weather . . . Friday will be the best day with a high of forty-nine degrees sometime between 1:00 and 3:00 p.m. Saturday is rain, Sunday is snow, and Monday and Tuesday both have highs in the thirties. So I guess we better get out there, wherever "there" is.
Charlie

I got a carbon fiber Trek 5200 road bike for Christmas, not too shabby for a first-time road bike. The bike only weighed seventeen pounds, so I knew it was going to be incredibly fast, especially on my favorite part—the downhill. I felt like *A Christmas Story*'s character Ralphie, who, in spite of everyone telling him he would shoot his eye out, got the perfect gift: the Red Ryder BB gun. Sam had a way of always being generous with gifts, but I was not expecting a top-of-the-line road bike. I was anxious about spending that much money before I was absolutely sure I was going to enjoy road biking. Sam was in his second year of his residency and we were not making very much money. He was always banking on the future of making the big bucks as a full-fledged doctor, but when he splurged like this, it worried me—plus, I was also feeling guilty, because deep down I knew the bike would get me what I wanted: more time with Ryann.

The first sight of the shiny charcoal bike against the wall was perfect, reflecting extra bright from the twinkling lights on the Christmas tree. I stood at the bottom of the steps, studying the view from afar with my eyes and mouth wide open, searching for words in my shock.

I finally began to speak out a cry that ended with a high squeak: "Ohhhh my gosh!"

I looked over at Sam and back at the bike, trying to determine which to hug first. Deciding that the former was much more important than a piece of carbon with two wheels, I ran to Sam, put my arms around him, and hugged with all my might. "Thank you, thank you, thank you! I love it!"

He gently and lovingly squeezed me back. "You're welcome. I know how you enjoy biking."

I immediately let go of him and slid across the room in my sock feet, resembling a dancing ice skater. As I closed in on the bike, I spoke over my shoulder: "But it must have been expensive."

"It wasn't too bad," he answered back.

Gliding right into the bike, I began to rub the top tube slowly, taking in the smooth finish. Then I put both hands on the lower drops of the handle bars and crouched down over the bike like I was already racing down a mountain and I wasn't going down it alone—Ryann was in front, leading the way.

In the background, my illusion of my first road bike ride was clouded by his words: "You're worth it, we can afford it, and besides, soon I will finish my residency, which means I will be making much more money."

A tingling flicker of shame shot down my back, but I disguised it well with a smile.

—

It took until late February before there was a day warm enough to get on my brand-new bike. But finally, Ryann called on a Monday and said, "The temperature should be in the high thirties or low forties tomorrow; anything above forty is tolerable for a road ride. Do you think you can handle it?"

Not wanting to show her my wimpy side, I said, "I'm ready! I've been waiting over two months to try out my new bike. I can hardly wait." Inside I was visualizing a red, aching, frozen nose, and numb ears and toes—but my speculation quickly dissolved into one thought: *I would put up with just about any kind of weather to spend time with her.*

She interrupted my thoughts with, "Do you have a balaclava?"

I swear I heard "baklava"—it was the only word I knew that was even close. I was already worried about not looking very intelligent to her, so this word completely threw me for a loop. I began to conjure up an explanation in my head—*maybe the combination of nuts and honey gives road cyclists magically high energy*—and answered back with doubt and questioning in my voice: "Does it make us ride faster?"

She replied, with as much (or more) doubt and questioning in her tone, "I guess the wind dynamics will help."

We paused for a moment, both silent, before I worked up the courage to say, "I think we are speaking of two different things."

She answered back with a fleeting giggle, "Did you think I was talking about baklava, the pastry we eat?"

A little, squeaky "yes" came out slowly.

I could feel the giggle I was falling in love with radiating through the phone as she said, "You silly girl, I was talking about a cap that looks like a ski mask we wear under our helmets to stay warm in the wind."

My pride a little wounded, I got defensive. "Well, if you would have just said ski mask; I didn't know you could call them baklava."

"It is a whole different word: *bal-a-cla-va*," she pronounced extra slow so I would hear the distinctive difference.

"Okay, I got it," I said. I didn't, but I figured I could look it up later. No reason to sound any dumber right now than I already felt I did.

———

The next day—armed with my brand-new black balaclava—I set out with Ryann for my first ride on my new road bike. It was freezing outside; the temperature on the car read thirty-nine degrees before we got out. So I put on my equipment and clothing really quickly to avoid getting too cold, knowing from experience with mountain biking that if my toes and fingers were cold before starting there was no way I would get them warm again.

I was on my third layer and getting ready to put on my fourth when Ryann smiled and said, "You're going to get hot and sweaty, and then you will get extremely cold when the wind hits your wet body. It's better to start out cold. And anyway, if you put that fourth layer on, you won't be able to move on the bike."

I paused with my jacket halfway up my arm. Feeling a bit embarrassed for being such a greenie, I said, "I know" and meekly pulled my arm back out of the sleeve.

Ryann was already dressed and ready to go when I was still busy putting on my balaclava, helmet, and clip-in shoes.

"Hurry up—it's best if we get moving," she said as she clipped one pedal in. With the crack of her clip floating in the air, I began to rush—so much so that I forgot one of the most important pieces of gear for biking in the cold: my windbreaker. I put my helmet on and saddled my bike quick as I could, clipped in one foot, and looked at her. "I'm ready. Let's go!"

"You will be if you straighten up that helmet," she said, smiling, and lightly tapped her own helmet. Then she swiftly pedaled away.

I looked at my reflection in the back window of her car. My helmet was extra crooked, leaning to the right side of my head. By the time I had it straightened out, Ryann was disappearing up the road. I hastily jumped on my bike as I got my other foot clipped in and pushed my pedals extra hard to try to catch up to her. This was a strategy that didn't work out so well for me, since my bike was in the big chain ring, which is the totally wrong gear for starting out on a steep incline. The combination of the high gear and my inexperience with clip-in road shoes overwhelmed me, and I fell over on my right hip.

The shoulder of the road was luckily full of grass and slightly damp mud, so I wasn't injured in the fall. I stole a look up ahead; Ryann hadn't seen me topple. A tenacious energy engulfed my psyche, and I started scrambling around to get up before she had a chance to witness my flip-flopping around on the ground. But my feet were still clipped securely into the pedals, and my legs were twisted up with the bike so tightly they resembled a pretzel. I was stuck.

"Damn it, damn it, damn it . . . I'm such a nincompoop . . . hurry up and get up, Carrie," I whispered to myself. I kept looking at Ryann's back as she pedaled in the distance and then back down at my feet; I was in a panic trying to quickly untangle myself from the bike. I felt like I was going to break my ankles in my frenzy. But finally, somehow, I managed to get one foot loose, which freed me up enough to get my other foot out. Then I made a straight upward leap into the air with my bike in hand and jumped over the saddle—just as I saw Ryann looking back to see where I was. I blew out a whistling exhalation of relief. *That was close!*

Barely clipped into the bike, I hastily yelled like a drunk who had just been caught relishing a tasty treat, "Just trying to get used to clipping in and out; no worries, I'll catch up!"

I sped up fast to catch her and started trailing her tire from behind. That little burst of exertion sent me into a turmoil of gulping for air. This was definitely going to use different muscles than I used on my mountain bike; I could feel the need for endurance more than quick surges of strength.

Ryann was looking back at me with questioning in her eyes. *Did she see me fall?*

"Was it hard to get clipped in and started? Because that can be the most difficult part for a new road biker to get used to," she said.

My embarrassment gave way to anger. "What do you expect without any directions?"

"I've learned it is best to let people figure this one out on their own," she said confidently, shrugging. "You can give way too many directions for clipping in, especially since not everyone has the same clips. Besides, most people who are new to clipping in experience at least a fall or two—it's just part of the learning curve."

"That makes sense . . . I guess," I said through my deep gulps for air.

I was only able to stay with Ryann for about half a mile and then I lost sight of her. I came around a switchback, and staring me right in the face was a gigantic hill with an extra-steep incline. To make matters worse, Ryann was effortlessly making her way over the crest, and this time in addition to looking back, she was peering *down* at me. My pride was collapsing; I hoped desperately that she couldn't sense my feeling of defeat.

Realizing I was going to have to downshift to make it up the hill, I stood and pushed with every bit of strength I had into my pedals while simultaneously shifting down. It was too late. I was already deep into the incline, and my bike went into a chain suck that abruptly froze my pedals in the middle of their revolution. Timbering through the air once again, I whispered desperately to myself, "Only me . . . yep, only me!"

This time I wasn't lucky enough to fall on a cushion of mud and grass; I crashed down onto hard pavement full of salt and pea gravel left over from the winter snow removal. I was able to liberate myself from my bike much more quickly than before and I immediately began fumbling with my chain.

I tried everything I could think of, and couldn't get the chain unstuck. Finally, as a last resort, I turned the bike upside down and pulled backward on the pedal. Voilà—the chain instantly released, hammering the pedal into the right side of my cheek. Seeing stars, I rubbed my cheek. When I had regained my composure, I jumped back onto my bike. As I did, the familiar sound of gears downshifting floated to my ears, extra sharp in the bitter cold. Ryann was coming back for me. My heart beat a hard little shiver of embarrassment.

As Ryann rolled up, she hollered with a puzzled look in her eyes, "Are you all right?"

Feeling the hot pain radiating from my cheek, I replied, "I'm fine, just a little cold and tired. Why do you ask?"

She turned around quickly and pulled up beside me. "Oh, I was just wondering."

I could hear the light, entertained chuckle in her voice and knew she had likely witnessed one of my falls, if not both of them.

"Did you see me fall?" I asked in a short, muffled voice.

"What?" she replied.

Content that she hadn't heard me, I said, "Nothing."

Ryann patted me on the back and pedaled up the hill. An excited tickle went through my whole body, reminiscent of the feeling I remember getting when I was a kid and was being chased in a game of tag. This energy helped me start pedaling again, despite my painfully bruised hips. There was no way I was going to get anywhere near her, but it was fun trying my best. And it seemed like she was enjoying the chase, too—keeping me just out of reach but within sight.

The fun started to subside when I read mile nine on my odometer and I couldn't see Ryann again. My muscles were quivering with fatigue, and I started to wonder if I would make it back to the car. I pulled over and stopped on the gravel shoulder alongside the road. There was a welcoming railroad track just a few feet away. I laid my bike down in the brown grass, awkwardly walked over to the tracks on my stiff road bike shoes—slightly twisting my ankles along the way—and sat down on one of the rails, hugging my knees in front of me.

The freezing metal immediately pierced through my winter spandex. In an effort to ignore the silent screams of pain emanating from my shivering body, I began humming out loud, staring off into the chilly West Virginia air. My mind trailed away to the thought of all the black coal that must pass along these rails on its way to heat homes in faraway places—a thought that made me wish deeply that I was in one of those warm homes at that very moment. There was a still quiet penetrating the air that made me think that more trains than cars must pass through this remote territory. The crisp stillness reinforced my hopes that West Virginia would stay undiscovered and manage to hold on to her secret beauty.

A crow cawing in the still, cold air just above me broke my agonized concentration, and I pulled an energy bar out of my jersey pocket. I tried to open it with my frozen fingers and had no success, so I used my teeth to angrily pry the wrapper open. My hunger, combined with my lackluster bike performance, was making me very frustrated. I would go no farther; I figured Ryann would come back when I didn't catch up or show up for a while.

The energy bar was just what I needed to settle my grumbling tummy down before Ryann appeared on the horizon, quickly making her way toward me. She looked spry and rested—the total opposite of how I was feeling. She rolled to a slow stop at my feet and asked once again, "Are you all right?"

This was no time to hold on to my pride, so I let out an exasperated sigh as I released my tight grip around my knees and put my hands on the icy tracks beside me. "I'm actually quite tired, and was kind of wondering if we could turn around now. I'm sure eighteen is not that far for you, but I'm a little worried I won't make it back to the car."

"Eighteen is a really good start," she said, though she sounded concerned. "I'm not sure if I even did that on my first ride."

"Cool. I was afraid you were going to think I was a big wimp because I was ready to turn around," I said.

"I'm good with turning around—and besides, it's really cold out. We have many more riding days in our future. And some may actually be when the sun is shining and the temps are above fifty!" Her mouth began to turn upward, and my quivering heart told me to look away from what was about to take place: her championship giggle.

I quickly looked down at the road, but was only able to focus on the salty pavement for a few nervous seconds before looking back up at her and getting caught in the middle of the giggle that was making me fall in love with her. I wasn't sure how I was falling for a smile, but it was clearly happening. I thought it had something to do with all the positive energy radiating outward from it. There are smiles, and then there are smiles loaded with piercing arrows full of purpose that can only be comprehended between lovers. At that moment, I felt sure we could cross boundaries and become lovers.

"I've been in the woods riding with you long enough to know you whine," Ryann said, still grinning, as she clipped in and started heading back to the car.

I stared at her back, noticing how her red curls peeked out of her helmet as she pedaled away. That image—it went deep. I stumbled to my feet and hopped over my bike to chase her once again. I was beginning to realize that there was a very confusing game going on between us: our athletic competition was morphing into uncharted love.

6
Mountains to Climb

I have traveled outside the mountains, but never lived apart from them. I always feared mountains would be as jealous, as unforgiving, as any spurned lover. Leave them and they may never take you back. Besides, I never felt a need to go. There is enough to study in these hills to last a lifetime.

—*Storming Heaven*, by Denise Giardina,
   born October 25, 1951, Bluefield, West Virginia

I was slowly chipping away the label of novice road rider, and hard black pavement was starting to take priority over dirt trails. This completely surprised me, since I took to road cycling like a fish flopping out of water—but once I finally relaxed and let the bike guide me, I started to open up to the advantages road cycling had to offer. I could get ready quicker and ride greater distances in a much shorter amount of time. It soon became totally natural for me to clip in and out of my pedals; I could do it without thinking, and with no more bruised hips or abrasions from clipping out at all the disastrously wrong moments. I took off the geek reflectors that come standard on new bikes—including the ones on the spokes of the tires, the ones I loved to watch go round and round as a child—and I stopped wearing underwear under my spandex to prevent unsightly lines and the awful chafing it caused in my most private areas. I was also beginning to acquire the obnoxious cycler's tan. In the nude, parts of me glowed with the illusion of wearing gloves, a wife-beater and painted-on '80s white jean shorts. My feet, which were always covered in the winter, shone extra brightly, like shiny glitter socks. It was enough to scare away any noncyclist.

From: Carrie
To: Charlie
Subject: Thanks for listening

Charlie,

You are always such a good listener. I must wear you out with my woes of my marriage and not understanding the direction my life is taking. I appreciate your understanding ear.

I'm going to take a break today and not ride my bike to work. My ankles and knees hurt from all the mountain biking I did yesterday, and I'm going to use them a lot today at work.
Carrie

From: Charlie
To: Carrie
Subject: Thanks for listening

Carrie,

I don't feel I did a very good job of listening or being supportive last night. I just get speechless when I hear the crazy things you are facing. I think I am better helping at math, but I am here to listen.

I did read a horoscope this morning that seems to fit you and your situation. "You're challenged over and over. You face each situation with a determination that equally matches your opposition's. Without force, and with great compassion, you'll rise as the victor."

Hang in there and you and your kids will make it just fine.
Charlie

Ryann and I were riding two to three days a week now. My summer was rich with bike rides and quaint, conversation-filled meals in Blacksburg. Between rides, we took the kids on hikes together in Camp Creek or out for a meal.

Ryann and I went through a couple of summer seasons before we began to understand the extent of what was going on between us. Then, one September, she invited me to go on a trip with her.

When my phone rang that day, my heart jumped a beat, just as it always did when Ryann's name lit up on the outside. I'm not sure why I had a feeling she could see me through the phone, but that's the way I was acting. I didn't answer on the first ring so I wouldn't appear too excited about speaking with her; I let my phone ring four times, before finally picking up and saying, "Hello?"

"Hey," she answered without hesitation. "What are you up to?"

"I'm having my morning coffee on the porch. Why, what are you doing?"

"Pretty much the same thing, but I had a question for you."

"Well, shoot away."

"I'm going to Athens, Georgia, in a couple of weeks. Do you think you could manage to get away and come along? We could get some riding in, and it is a really nice place to visit, good food and good coffee."

My eyelids jumped and I swallowed a gulp of air that was somehow waxing and waning between bliss and melancholy. My mom's oft-repeated words—"Remember, Carrie, you can't turn back the hands of time"—began reverberating in time with my nervous heart. I wanted to run with my blissful feeling, embrace it, and live with it, but I knew, or at least thought, I belonged here in this home with Sam and the boys.

I held the phone tight to my ear. *What am I going to do? Go to Georgia or not?* I wasn't sure. Hoping she couldn't hear the disappointment in my voice that she wasn't inquiring about a ride today, I said, "Oh, I don't know. . . . Maybe I could go visit my sister in Atlanta and then come back through Athens. It would have to be a quick trip for me, probably only the weekend and an extra day or two to get back. I would also have to convince Sam to get the boys to and from school until I get back. I'm not sure he'll go for it."

"Well, see what you can work out and let me know in the next day or two."

I was already thinking up ways in my head to convince Sam I deserved this much-needed break. "Okay. I'll run it past him and let you know what he says." Then, before Ryann could hang up, I blurted out, "Can you ride this weekend any time?"

"I think I can Sunday, but let me see what Alex's schedule is like."

"Check on it and let me know as soon as you have it figured out. I would love to get out for a ride this weekend."

There was a pause and silence before our good-byes awkwardly stumbled over one another and we hesitantly hung up.

———

Sam got home late that evening from work; the boys were already bathed and watching a movie in the family room. He went upstairs to change before he came down, and we said our quick hellos with a mutual kiss on the cheek as we passed on the steps in different directions. I knew he would eat and play with the boys for a while before bedtime, so I went to catch up on laundry.

About an hour later I could hear little boy jabber mixed with his deep voice as he read to the boys in their room, which was next to ours. I was already in bed, drifting in and out of sleep and full of worried thoughts of how separated our lives had become. My life was busy with the boys and enjoying my new friendship with Ryann, along with my newfound love for road cycling. Sam, meanwhile, was working hard on his medical career, which meant extended hours at the hospital or office. Most of the free time we did have together we spent with the boys, which left little time for our needs as a couple.

I was pondering all this as Sam slipped quietly under the sheets and lightly put his fingers on the curve of my hip—an inquiring touch. I clinched my eyes closed and made a disapproving moan as if I was sleeping, but I was very aware of his presence. It was a ritual we'd been repeating for weeks, one that always ended with me rolling away from him and peeking through squinted eyes out the window, hoping he would become exhausted with trying and give up. But tonight I wanted to ask about Athens, so I finally gave in to his desires: I made hollow, deceptive love with him.

When we were done, before Sam could turn over and fall asleep, I mustered up the courage to ask. It wouldn't come as a complete surprise, since Ryann and I were spending lots of time together riding bikes, but I thought it would be best to give him the question in bits.

"I want to go see my sister Kim in a couple of weeks," I said.

"Sure."

A murmur of relief came over me, because at least now I knew I could go to Georgia. Twisted up with that relief was a feeling of bitterness, however; I felt like a child asking for something from a parent. I ignored that thought for the time being. Now it was time to work on the other bits of the question. "Ryann will be in Athens and I thought about stopping on the way home to ride with her."

Sam's reply was abrupt and laced with anger. "When is this, exactly? How are you going to be able to ride bikes with the boys?"

My heart started to drop a little, but I knew there was still hope, so I persevered. "You just said I could go, didn't you? I was hoping to make it a long weekend and leave the boys with you. It's not this weekend but the next. You would only have to get them to and from school on Friday."

He promptly turned to face away from me and pulled the covers over his shoulder. "Whatever," he mumbled. "Go ahead."

———

The following Sunday, Ryann and I went biking in Newport, Virginia. The loop included a ride up to the top of Mountain Lake—a total distance of thirty-three miles, with the halfway point being a considerably difficult climb up to Mountain Lake Hotel via State Route

613. A great deal of the movie *Dirty Dancing* was filmed at the nearly one-hundred-year-old lodge and surrounding lake in the 1980s.

Ryann had done this ride several times, and I was always putting it off because of the strenuous average grade of 11 percent, which got up to 16 percent the last five miles on 613 to the top of the mountain. The payoff was the screaming downhill on State Route 700 after a bathroom break at the lodge. Sometimes I wondered if we put ourselves through torturous hill climbs because it made all the other difficulties we deal with in life seem so easy by comparison. This one sounded particularly difficult. But I finally agreed to do the ride with Ryann if she would be patient and wait on me at the top.

Before we got out of the car, Ryann began to feed my cycling ego. "I knew you were going to be a natural at road biking. You've improved so much in so little time."

"Yeah, right," I responded, even though I knew what she was saying had some truth to it. At least now I was able to keep her in sight when we rode together and the majority of our time riding was spent beside one another. I was still losing her on the hill climbs, but I could catch up to her on the downhills. I had no reason to add braking to my repertoire of cycling skills, since I had not yet experienced a downhill wreck.

As the climbing began on 613 up to Mountain Lake, a light drizzle began to come down and we were still in talking distance of one another.

"Go ahead," I told Ryann. "I'll find you at the top."

"Okay," she yelled over her shoulder, nodding. "If I stop, I won't be able to get back on my bike, and if I go much slower, I think I might turn over. I'll be waiting in the lodge. Try to make it without getting off your bike." With that, she stood and pedaled on up the treacherous mountain, leaving me behind.

"I will," I whimpered, between heavy breaths.

She became the size of a pea and then disappeared around a sharp switchback. I could feel the weakness settle into my quads in the first mile of the climb. There was no one to talk to, so I concentrated on my breathing and trying to make it symmetrical and deep while watching the thick woods inch by. I began to think of all the people who rode up this road year after year in the famous Mountains of Misery Road Ride, with close to 10,000 feet of climb in just over one hundred miles. This last hill stretch was the finish to the ride; the fatigue must be unbearable with a hundred miles under your belt. *I could use some company in my misery now*, I thought, wishing Ryann had waited for me.

Logically, I knew there was no actual correlation between my sluggish speed and the rain, but it seemed like the slower I climbed the stronger the drizzle came down. My cheap rain jacket started sticking to me and the water penetrated through to my skin, especially my arms. I began sniveling to myself with every outward breath, "You can do this. . . . You can do this. . . . I know you can." I felt like a kid trying to motivate myself with thoughts of the Little Engine That Could chugging down the track. But I was still questioning whether I was going to make it to the top of the mountain without getting off my bike.

I looked at my bike computer and the grade hit 14 percent, then it went down to 11, and then back up to 15 in what seemed like a few hundred feet. I came around a switchback and saw an inviting guardrail on the side of the road, and that was that: just as quick as I saw it, I unclipped from my bike and stumbled over to an area protected by some trees that seemed to be dryer than anywhere else in the vicinity. I put my bike up against it and sat down on the thick, heavy metal of the railing. I knew there would be another opportunity to try to make it to the top—and next time I would make every effort to keep Ryann beside me. I had no idea then that the following year I would have built up enough strength and stamina to ride the sixty-four-mile option of the Mountains of Misery ride while Ryann rode the hundred-mile version.

I looked up at the sky to see the falling rain getting heavier by the minute. The incoming drops deflected off my helmet, onto my nose, and ended their descent into my mouth. It was salty-tasting, and I knew my sweat was being washed away. Unfortunately, my fatigue wasn't going away with it. Weariness had infiltrated my legs, and I needed an antidote—specifically, rest—to take it away. My body was starting to shiver.

The rhythmic chatter of the rain dripping from the leaves was interrupted by a distant clash of thunder. I jumped high from the rail out of fear and, after leaping back on my bike, started pedaling on the wet pavement up the mountain once again. But no sooner had I started my revolutions than my legs decided to collapse. I gave in to my exhaustion and started to walk my bike up the steep sections, riding only when I was able. The thunder was getting closer, so my walking turned into a brisk run, which is not easy to do on stiff platform road bike shoes with metal clips protruding from the sole. I resembled someone who was learning to skate for the first time: legs slipping away from one another, stumbling, trying desperately to hold on to my bike even as I slid on the slick pavement. I almost fell twice but recovered just before landing on the hard road. Each time it happened, I frantically scanned the woods and road around me to see if anyone was witnessing my awkward dance.

I finally made it to the entrance of the lodge about thirty minutes after Ryann and I separated on our climb up the mountain. I was riding slowly, just barely turning the crank enough to keep the bike upright, as I was still trying to recover from the climb.

I could see her from a distance leaning on one of the rock archways that faced the lake with her bike sitting against the wall just inside. She looked rested and content, with no worries. It occurred to me at that moment that she seemed to be happiest when she was biking. I thought maybe it was for the same reason I felt only bliss when pedaling on my bicycle: riding offered a short escape from a life I didn't know how to handle.

I hung my head low as I came in under the shelter of the stone archway. Dripping with rain and sweat, I got off my bike and leaned it against hers, trying my best to hide my heavy breathing.

"Hey, sorry it took me so long to get here," I sighed out between gulps of breath.

"It's okay. Don't worry—I've done this ride so many more times than you. Did you make it all the way without getting off your bike?"

My competitive edge almost took over and I thought about lying, but I decided against it. Cyclists like to be able to say, "I've done this mountain or that mountain" because it gives them bragging rights or a sense of accomplishment, but I was feeling somewhat defeated at the moment.

"No," I said, looking down at the wet ground. "I tried really hard, but my legs just wouldn't listen to what my mind was saying and I had to get off and rest." In a much lower voice I added, "I also walked some of the way up." Turning back to where I had just come from, I pointed my arm straight out with intent. "That mountain is really hard; I'm surprised I'm even here."

"No worries—you made it one way or another, and you're here with me under shelter and out of the rain. Let's wait it out here for a bit and see if it slows down."

"Thanks. It helps to know you haven't given up on me yet. I'm sure with a little more riding time I'll be able to make it up without getting off my bike." I clasped my hands behind my back and leaned my shoulders into the chilly rocks behind me. The rain made the river rocks wet, sending a frigid shiver from my head to my toes. We stood facing one another, framed under the stone archway. "Waiting here for a while sounds like a great idea to me. I'm not too keen on getting any wetter, my feet are soaked, and I'm cold. Aren't you cold without a raincoat on?"

"No," Ryann said. "I had a rhythm going up the hill, and I didn't want to stop to put mine on."

I put both hands on my hips and forced my chest into an accusatory pose. "I think the correct term for that 'hill' is 'mountain.'"

"Well, ex*cuse* me," she shot back with a wink.

I was trembling on the outside, but felt entirely warmhearted on the inside—full of affection for Ryann. I knew she couldn't have been standing there long, because the raindrops running down her arms were full drops and had just slightly begun to blend her freckles together. I started to daydream I was running my finger down the wet drops along her arm to her hands, about to interlock our fingers, but just as I was contemplating pulling her close to me, she interrupted my delusional thoughts and startled me awake.

"Are you going to be able to make the trip to Athens?"

I wondered if she had any idea what I had been so intently thinking about as I was staring at her arms. "Yes, but it was a little difficult to convince Sam. I have to come back on Sunday."

She was smiling. "I'm going to leave on Thursday with Alex so we have a good amount of time visiting with my aunt. Call when you get there and we can go out for dinner or something."

I felt a little giggle inside and smiled much bigger than her, thinking of how wonderful it would be to spend time alone with her in a city where we would be strangers to the locals. *Who knows?* I thought. *I might be able to act on my delusional daydreaming and actually hold her hand in public.* I glanced down and scooted a pebble around with the tip of my shoe, suddenly feeling shy. When I awkwardly looked back up, my eyes made contact with her again, but very timidly. "Sounds like a plan. I've been there once before, when Sam was checking out residency programs, and there's a really nice vegetarian restaurant called the Grit; it's a little like Gillie's in Blacksburg. What do you think about going there?"

"I love vegetarian. Let's try it," she said.

"Okay. I'll call when I get there and we can meet each other."

The rain was composing a lovely orchestra around us, making distinctly different sounds as each drop collided with the puddles, lake, trees, and metal roof of the lodge. We stood for about another hour under the archway, waiting until the rain tapered to a slight drizzle, and once again we forgot the world outside us and our bikes.

7
Athens, Georgia

What is hard to remember when you're in the middle of it is that when you get through to the other side, you always walk away with a gift. If you can stand in there and not walk away from it, you get transformed by it.

—Kathy Mattea, born June 21, 1959, South Charleston, West Virginia

The morning of my trip, I woke shortly after Sam left for work and hurried the boys to get ready before dropping them at school. Ryann and Alex were already in Athens, visiting with her aunt. Atlanta was too far and would take too much time, so my plans changed: I would head straight to Athens. I tossed my last bag in the back of the car and locked my bike on the rack, and as soon as I stepped in behind the wheel, a giddy, happy feeling—one laced with a bit of guilt—filled my mind. I blew up my cheeks and let out a heavy sigh as I started the engine, telling myself to ignore the guilt that was eating away at me.

From: Carrie
To: Charlie
Subject: Yesterday

Charlie,

I'm sorry I was so blunt about joining the lesbian support group at All Souls—I'm just not ready. I'm still uncertain about what I want. I spoke to my therapist and we are going to meet

a couple more times and he may refer me to someone else. My
mind is so full of confused alphabet soup and he told me this
is the nature of counseling—it stirs us up, and helps empty out
our souls so we can attempt to see clearly. He told me to keep
in mind that people come and go as needed. So I think I will
attend a few more sessions. I don't know just where I'm going,
but I'm gonna try to figure it out . . . a little at a time.

Thanks for caring,
Carrie

From: *Charlie*
To: *Carrie*
Subject: *Yesterday*

Carrie,

I think you are very mature (more than I am) and very
smart in many ways, but sometimes lack the self-esteem to
stand your ground. I do care enough to want you to take better
care of yourself and I will continue to push for that.

I like the fact that you are pushing back on my simplistic
solutions. You are learning to stand up for your reality, which
is much more complicated than I want to believe.

It looks like the year to come will be bringing more growth
for you.

Hang in there,
Charlie

I made one quick stop for lunch on the way down to Athens; I was
too excited to linger on the road for very long. I arrived in Athens
around two and checked into the Foundry Park Inn before going
downtown to explore it in a different light than I had the first time
with Sam, when I'd had mostly his medical residency in mind.

Four or five years had passed since I had been there, and the

Georgia Bulldog statues that lined the streets—each one decorated by a different artist with a different theme—were new to me. I walked down the brick sidewalks along College Street, past the bulldog Caesar Dawgustus, who was clad in his red Greek toga and sandals, and I lingered above him for a few minutes, breathing in the sights and sounds of the vibrant college town, before I turned to go into Starbucks, hoping caffeine would keep my energy going and hold the sleep I so desperately needed on the back burner.

Coffee in hand, I walked up and down the eclectic shop-lined downtown, observing the diverse population around me: students, families, and businesspeople. The scene took me back to Western Carolina, where I met Sam. We began dating in my first year of college, when I was extremely naive and had no clear understanding as to what direction my future was going to take. Sam and I were inseparable for the next two and a half years, until he went away to medical school in West Virginia. When I graduated less than a year later, we got married and I joined him up north. There was no time to think if I was making the right decision—I just knew I had made it and I was sticking with it.

Out of the corner of my eye, I saw a store overflowing with vividly colored crafty items, lotions, soaps, and clothes that looked to be original, not the chain-store variety. I wandered in and recognized the sweet smell of lavender and patchouli swirling in the air. A charming shirt in the back of the store caught my eye and I stopped thinking of Sam and clouded my mind with Ryann again. The harder I tried to seize control of my thoughts of Ryann, the more I wondered if she would think I was pretty in the shirt. I wove through the bright colors and soft scents to the back of the room, pulled out a medium, and stood in front of the mirror as I held it under my chin and against my breast. It was beautiful, and it made me feel a long-lost innocence, like I was going to spend an evening with a first love—a real love, not one I awkwardly tried to convince myself of. Ever since my adolescence, I had been trying to write another story with my life, a false one—and that included my marriage, which was feeling more and more like a chore that I merely tolerated with every day that passed.

I decided then and there that this was the shirt I was going to wear to the Grit that evening. I could barely contain my excitement as I grabbed the shirt, put it under my arm, and dashed to the front of the store to purchase it. I danced a little on the way out the door with happy anticipation, thinking of the evening ahead.

—

I tried to take a nap back at my hotel, but was unsuccessful; I just stared at the ceiling, wondering why I was there and not back home in West Virginia with my family. What was this volatile feeling I was struggling to tame?

The commotion in my mind stopped the instant the hotel phone rang loudly, rattling the bedside table. I rolled over and, tucking a pillow under my head to sit up a bit, brought the phone to my ear. "Hello?"

"How was your trip down?" I was relieved to hear Ryann's voice, not Sam's, on the line.

"Uneventful. I got here around two and strolled around downtown for a while, and then I came to the hotel and tried to take a nap, but I wired myself with so much coffee I couldn't sleep a wink."

"Are you still up for dinner at the Grit tonight?" she asked.

"Sure. What time were you thinking?"

"Say six?"

I looked at the clock; a brightly illuminated 4:33 was staring back at me. "That will work for me, but I guess I better get up now and take a shower."

"I'll swing by a little before six," she said.

"I'll be here."

"Okay, I'll see you in a few."

"Bye."

As soon as I heard the click echo on the other end, the silence of my room surrounded me, accompanied by a dizzy confusion. I sat up on the side of the bed and thought about calling Sam to let him know I had arrived, but I was afraid he would recognize the anxiety I was feeling in my voice, so I decided I would call later—or tomorrow.

I took an extra-long, hot shower, hoping the heat would melt away the thrilling but painful energy I was feeling. As I stepped away from the steam surrounding me to peer at my naked body in front of the barely visible mirror, I reached for the towel that was hanging over my head and pulled it in front of my face. Then I held it there for a moment and took in a few deep breaths before letting out a sighing plea to myself: "Just stop thinking and you'll be okay."

Realizing I was going to be late if I didn't stop looking for answers at the moment, I quickly got the rest of the way ready. I put on my new shirt and stood admiring it in the mirror for what seemed like an interminable five minutes, hypnotized by the stripes running down its front, once again contemplating what was going on in my mind and heart. When would I ever stop looking for answers?

At a quarter till six, a light *tap, tap* on the door interrupted my last thought: *You're in deeper than you realize.*

"Coming!" I called, as I skipped across the room. I pulled the door ajar and stared out at Ryann, who was facing the opposite direction. As soon as I saw her, the feelings of enchantment overshadowed my guilty ones. She turned around and we locked eyes for a moment. It took me back to that day in the garden when she brought the rack over to my house. Just as it had then, our desire felt tangible. *Stop, Carrie, stop*, I told myself, as I said, "Hey" out loud.

"Are you ready?" she asked.

I pulled the door closed behind me. "Yep, let's go eat."

———

We made it to the Grit a few minutes after six. The aroma of global spices simmering along with sweet baked goods was blowing in the breeze just outside the door, and it increased threefold as we stepped inside. There was a nutty curry smell in it that reminded me of my childhood summers at my grandma Cornell's house. She was always baking goodies and trying international recipes, and the smells seeped out the windows as I played outside.

We sat down and ordered our food, and then it felt like invisible walls closed the two of us into our own little world. Despite the busy restaurant moving around us, it was just us. We talked incessantly about our children, husbands, gardening, biking, careers, and how life would have been different without children or husbands. Well over an hour went by with us tightly caught up in conversation that I didn't notice time passing, until Ryann hit me with the inevitable question that we had both been avoiding.

"Have you ever thought of being with a woman romantically?" Her voice was brave and nonchalant, like it was an everyday question.

I felt my cheeks flush. *How can she ask a question of that magnitude so easily?* I took a sip of ice water to defer answering, but it backfired on me and I shocked myself into a slight gargle before I choked out, "Excuse me?"

I don't know why I acted as though it blindsided me; unspoken passion had been lingering between us for months like thick steam. But I wasn't sure I was ready to answer her question.

Ryann was relentless; with more energy in her voice, she said, "You heard me. Have you ever thought of being with a woman romantically?"

I glanced at her, then back down to my water, searching for the perfect words. I twisted the straw between my fingers and scanned the busy restaurant before leaning forward and timidly answering slightly above a whisper, "Yes, I've been wondering about it since I was a teenager, but now that I've met you, I think about it at least once a day—maybe more."

Her eyes twinkled like a burst of tiny fireworks, and just as she was going to say something, the waitress showed up at our table with the check. "Are you ready for your bill?"

We looked at each other with half smiles before overlapping one another with giggles. The waitress was hovering above us with puzzled eyes and no words.

Ryann filled in the questioning air. "Yes, please."

I could have sworn I saw the waitress roll her eyes slightly as she set the check down on our table before walking away. I didn't blame her—we must have looked like two teenagers poking fun at something. I looked back at Ryann, and my stomach knotted up inside with wonder and fear. I was alone with her again, and now the question that had been hanging between us was finally open for discovery.

We drove back to the hotel in silence. I think we both were afraid of bringing up Ryann's question again for fear we would act on it. I was wishing that I had driven myself to the restaurant so I could run back to my room alone and hide.

Ryann parked the car outside the hotel and we remained voiceless: I sat staring at my lap and she peered out the window. I felt like an awkward teenager about to act on my first kiss.

I ended the silence with what I knew had to come next: "Would you like to come in for a bit?" *Oh my, you didn't just ask her to come into your empty hotel room, did you, Carrie? Yes, you did. And what do you think might happen in there?* Like a sassy teenager, I responded to those thoughts with a snappish *Maybe what* should *happen.*

Ryann looked at me as if she could see and understand everything about me, and without hesitation, she answered, "Yes, I would like to come in."

That was it—no more pretense at a "happily ever after" life. The facades we had created at home were crumbling, and I think we both knew it. We exited the car, and our cadence across the parking lot was as slow as if we were going to a funeral. We were silent as we entered my room, but our desire was so thick we almost had to swim across the threshold.

I picked up the remote and clicked on the television, then strategically placed myself on the edge of the bed in case I came to my senses and needed to make a quick getaway. Ryann perched herself near me. Spastic with excitement, I started changing the channels, flying through them. I thought if I switched the stations fast enough, the images I was seeing of my family—visions of Sam and the boys, superimposing themselves over the screen—would vaporize. It didn't work; channel after channel, all I could see were the faces of my loved ones. But they were back home and I was here in Athens, Georgia, on a bed with someone I was falling in love with.

I closed my eyes and shook my head slightly, begging the images to go away. I had always prided myself on my loyalty, but my senses were telling me something different right now, and I couldn't restrain them. Ryann was an irresistible temptation that I wanted to put to rest.

Ryann moved on the bed a little without saying anything, and it startled me to my feet. Realizing what I'd done, I sat back down just as fast as I'd risen, feeling embarrassed. My body and mind were spinning inside and out with a blurry, feverish panic. I stopped on a channel with a symphony program that seemed to be a Latin composer introducing "O Fortuna."

Ryann calmly put her hand on my shoulder, and my family disappeared from the screen. My initial reaction was stiffness from fright, but little by little I collapsed into her hand, which was gently pulling me back to her. The enthralling chorus echoed with the beating of our hearts as our bodies became lost in a labyrinth with one another. Late into the twilight, my flesh lost all capacity for reason under her ability to touch me in a way I'd never imagined possible. Her sweetness that evening was my truth integrated with my cowardice. Each time she touched me with her soft fingertips, the electricity it sparked made me more aware of how inevitable this encounter had been all along. Once you give another person the deep abyss of your emotions—a place that no one else has seen or felt—it's impossible to forget. How could I ever turn back? Our night disappeared into a soft, warm velvet sunshine we created for one another. Our souls joined together and floated outside on the shadows of the Georgia night—to our families in West Virginia, to the stars and the moon, and back.

———

Ryann left around two so she would be home for her aunt and Alex in the morning. I walked her to the door and we avoided too many questions, for fear of no answers.

"Good night," I said.

She flashed me her beautiful smile, along with a wink, and said, "Night. I'll be by here around nine and we can go ride our bikes." Then, in a lower voice, she said, "By the way, it was your shirt that sent me over the edge."

I smiled back at her with pursed lips and whispered with the little breath I had left, "Bravo."

I shut the door slowly as Ryann walked away, closing the cool night air out with her. I dragged my feet on the carpet before sluggishly climbing back into bed. I begged for sleep to come, but it was hopeless—her scent was everywhere, between the sheets and on my skin, and it was keeping my mind delirious, torn between remorse and passion. I darted in and out of restless slumber the entire night, searching for an easy answer to one question: *What have I just done?*

At seven I decided I couldn't lie in bed wide awake, trying to answer dead-end questions any longer. I felt like I had gotten a total of one hour of sleep the whole night. I was completely exhausted from the question that was now first in my mind: *What next?* My stomach was twisted with turmoil. I felt as if I'd been in fight-or-flight mode for hours. I didn't want to lose my family, but I didn't want to lose Ryann, either.

I went in the bathroom and turned to the mirror. Looking at myself, I first felt disgust, quickly followed by an uneasy nervousness and last a newfound excitement. A single tear crawled down my face as I tried to figure out who this person staring back at me was. I had no idea who I had become.

I leaned my exhausted weight against the sink and watched the tear rolling down my cheek until it fell from my chin and disappeared into the drain. Perhaps this was the real me today, and before last night, a stranger had been living in my body.

8
Comin' Up a Storm

*I feel my fear moving away in rings through time for a
million years.*

—Breece D'J Pancake, born June 29, 1952,
   South Charleston, West Virginia

Ryann came early to the hotel room, as promised, for our bike ride.
I reached for both her hands when she came in and gave them a
modest squeeze as I pulled her to me. She returned my kiss, but reluctantly, it seemed to me. She smiled as we parted, and I grinned slightly
back. Then she backed away to sit on the chair in the corner while
I got dressed for our bike ride. We were silent, and I moved around
her gingerly until I mustered up the courage to ask the question I had
been pondering all night: "What now?"

To: Charlie
From: Carrie
Subject: The library

Charlie,

*Thanks for taking me to the library; I think it will be a good
place for me to escape in the future and write. Also thanks for
the feedback on Quinn and me. Just know that I do hear and so
appreciate it. It may seem that I have a hard shell, but I really
don't, or maybe it's the other way around. . . . I try to appear*

that I have a hard outer shell, but inside I see my limitations and I get scared about my future. I somehow have to overcome these fears and move forward. (I'm working on it—I promise.) It's nice to know that someone has faith in me.

I think Quinn has a great chance to reach his goals, so thanks for helping me help him to achieve them. He will have struggles, but this will build a much better person to handle other conflicts he may encounter along the way.

Thanks again for dinner. It was nice. And don't forget to read.
Carrie

To: Carrie
From: Charlie
Subject: The library

Carrie,

I did not mean to become impatient with your whining. I just need to adjust to a more passive listening role. If my listening to whining helps you, by all means, whine away.

And I appreciate your encouragement for me to get back to reading. You might be helping me more than I am helping you. Someday you will need to write a book on your life. You appear to be an island of calm in the middle of rough seas.
Charlie

"What now?"

It was such a big question; it filled the room with intimidating energy that neither one of us knew how to handle. I think we were both thinking the same thing but afraid to be the first to answer. But the desire I felt for her was still speaking to me with such fervor. I wanted to embrace her tightly in my arms and acknowledge what both of us were feeling. Each heavy beat of my heart reverberated like thunder, sending fear into my throat. I looked at her anxiously; her expression mirrored mine.

I stretched out across the bed and put both hands close to her without actually touching her and asked again: "What now?"

Ryann leaned toward me, put her elbows on her thighs, and clasped her hands together on her knees. She was all business. "Nothing has changed," she said firmly. "Someone who loves you very much made love with you. Don't make a big deal out of it."

With dismay in my voice, I reached for her hands and squeezed them. "How do you move on and not make a big deal out of this? Not only does my mind feel deceptive, I feel it all over my whole body. I not only had an affair, it was with a woman. What does that say about who we are, Ryann?"

"Carrie we really don't need to feed the situation; let's just go for a bike ride and figure things out later."

"But we have to go home to our families and act as though nothing has happened," I pleaded.

"Yes, we do, but I don't suppose either one of us is too keen on leaving them."

The guilt I was holding inside was so overwhelming and torturous, I wanted to fix it right then. I knew once we got on our bikes we would focus on riding and forget the topic of our affair. I couldn't understand how she could compartmentalize and move on so quickly. I was losing my words in the burning pit of my emotions. But I decided that if she was unwilling to work through them with me now, I would try to be strong and save them for later also. I felt absolutely sure there was no possible way we could forget our night together. It was a memory of a lifetime for me, ranking up there with all my other major life transitions: getting married, having my boys, and losing my first family member. This would remain with me and change me forever, and I hoped Ryann would be part of that change.

"Okay, let's go." I let go of her hands and rolled over to the end of the bed, jumped up, grabbed my bike, and headed for the door. As I passed through, Ryann came right up behind me and squeezed out next to me, but without touching me. I could feel that familiar magnetic energy between us as she passed, but neither of us acted on it. I wanted to scream, to embrace her with all my might, but I couldn't find the strength, so I just let her pass by.

—

Ryann navigated around Athens and I stayed as close to her back tire as possible to let her pull my numb body and mind along. There was too much wind out for us to have a conversation—or at least we both knew it was a good excuse not to talk. So we rode along with only the sound of the breeze and our changing gears to break the silence. It was the longest two-hour ride of my life; it dragged on and on as hundreds of questions with no answers blossomed in my mind.

Back at the hotel, Ryann helped me get my gear in the room, but she seemed frantic and uncomfortable. As soon as she set my bag inside the door, she turned to leave. "I'm going to go now, Carrie."

I let go of my bike and it hit the wall with a clash. Before it had a chance to topple all the way to the floor, I blurted out, "That's it—nothing more?"

She answered with what sounded like exasperation. "What more can we do, Carrie—make love again? That would just make us want more. We should just let this tiny little blurb disappear."

I was taken aback for a moment. I dropped my arms to my side and my eyes widened with protest. "A 'tiny little blurb'?" I asked. "Is that all last night meant to you?"

"Compared with what we have back home, yes, that is what I would call it. Why should we erode the safe walls that we've created?"

"Because I don't want our love to disappear anymore, Ryann. Home may seem safe, but it's not real."

Ryann seemed to be full of knowledge that I lacked. My naive romantic ideals that we could somehow open up our secret love couldn't stand up to her cold realism. She knew there was not much we could change at that moment—so why, she reasoned, should we perpetuate it by sleeping together again? Neither one of us was ready to talk about wiping out the history of our families. Our best choice was to be quiet and let the situation fizzle out.

I was less willing to accept this than she was. I kept hoping we could find a way to act on our newfound energy.

"Carrie, I'm going," she said with little emotion, turning her head back only slightly toward me before descending the steps. It was as though in hiding her face she was trying to disguise her thoughts.

All I could hear were my own voices of desperation, but I couldn't get them out. I leaned against the doorjamb, heavy with guilt and fear, and watched her walk away. I couldn't look away. I was sure she was thinking that with each determined step she took, this "tiny little blurb" would be that much easier to erase—certainly easier than extricating herself from her life back home. It took every bit of my might to constrain my feet from bounding down the steps after her. I felt nauseous; my stomach churned, and in my imagination I saw myself running after her, grabbing her by the shoulders, turning her around, and convincing her how important it was for us to be with one another.

The heavy snowstorm rising inside my chest culminated with the shutting of her car door.

I heard her key turn in the ignition, and I staggered down beyond the door and began carelessly walking toward her car—until I realized I was crying uncontrollably and stopped myself. I watched her drive away, but didn't once see her eyes move from the road to look in her rearview mirror.

I turned to go back into my hotel room with the overwhelming feeling that I wouldn't be able to calm myself for quite some time. Inside, as I looked around the room, I realized I must remove myself from the scene of the crime. I collected my things, made two hasty trips to the car, and checked out.

I hadn't been able to eat much breakfast, and it was past lunch time, so I was hoping to eat a little before heading back to West Virginia. I aimlessly wandered the sidewalks of Athens until I stumbled upon The Bluebird Café and decided it would do: you could get breakfast all day there, and I was sure breakfast food was all my churning stomach could handle.

There were only a few people inside eating, so I strategically headed for the lonely table in the back corner of the room, attempting to hide my emotional state.

A waitress who didn't look much over twenty-five came right away to take my order. She was beautiful, with only a small amount of makeup around her eyes. Her hair was blonde, and her brown eyes had a welcoming, considerate look about them. She peered down at me and asked, "Coffee?" in a voice barely above a whisper, as if she knew I'd chosen a quiet spot for a reason. Her Southern accent was thick, like she'd grown up on one of those deep Georgia back roads where Spanish moss hangs low from the ancient live-oak trees.

I looked her directly in the eyes. "Yes, that would be wonderful."

"You need a minute to look over the menu?"

"I think so."

She wrote something on her pad, then walked back to the kitchen. Watching her go, I thought to myself, *She's kinda cute—I wonder if she's ever been with a woman.* I assumed this would be the question in my head each time I encountered a woman for days to come. It was a question I'd been asking myself for years, but after what had happened the night before, I knew it would be visiting my mind more and more.

The waitress promptly returned with coffee. "You about ready to order?"

"Yes—I'm not feeling too well, so I think I'll have one scrambled egg, grits, and a biscuit with apple butter." It was the blandest thing I could find on the menu.

"Okay," she said with a smile. "I'll be back in a bit."

I watched her walk away and I had to quiet my inquiring mind once again. I felt the heat of every swallow of coffee go down as I waited and tried to understand the anger I was beginning to feel toward myself for succumbing to my desires. I cradled the warm mug in my hands and held it to my forehead, hoping it would heat my mind out of its busy, regretful chatter. I kept repeating with a slight whisper to myself over and over, "What am I going to do? How can I go home?"

"Excuse me, your food." The waitress startled me awake.

"Oh, thank you." My hand shook as I put the mug down, and I spilled some coffee on the place mat. My eyes were watery and blood-shot; I was sure I looked like I'd spent all night in a local bar drinking.

The waitress reached inside her apron, pulled a rag out, and started dabbing up the coffee. "Bad night?"

I had no inhibition at the moment, probably because of lack of sleep, combined with the hurt I was feeling in my heart. *I'm sure I'll never see her again; what do I have to lose?* So I looked right up into her cute brown eyes and without any reservations I said, "I guess you could say I'm bad and my night was not too far from bad. I slept with a woman last night, and I have a husband and two boys back home waiting on me, but I really don't feel much like going home." My voice was shaking by the end of my confession.

The waitress gazed with intensity into my eyes before taking a cautious look around the room. Next she bit her bottom lip and brought that penetrating gaze right back to me. I started to think I had made a mistake and shocked her so much that she had lost her voice. But as she put my food on the place mat in front of me, she said without any hesitation in her statement, "Oh, honey, most of us have experimented with women a time or two in our lives—but you look sick, really sick, like you saw death last night."

I looked at my food. Warm steam rose slowly from it; it looked like a ghost escaping. "I think I did see death . . . of my life as I knew it," I said.

Her mouth dropped open, and she fell silent.

I decided to say exactly what I was feeling: "I think I might be gay."

She didn't bother to check around the room this time before she muttered, with a little worry in her voice, "I reckon maybe you oughta go home and forget this ever happened. Probably be best for everyone, including yourself. Being gay is not an easy life, and you sound like you have a family to take care of back home."

The smell of the warm food before me was comforting, but the girl's comments made me feel like I should have just kept my mouth closed. My eyes shied away from hers, and I looked out the window to examine the traffic passing by. "I don't know if I want to forget or even if I can no matter how hard I try," I said. "I made love to someone I've been in love with for a really long time, and no one was there to tell me it was wrong because it was a woman. It's been a long time coming—a really long time."

I was utterly shocked at myself for even starting this whole conversation; it was very out of the ordinary for me. The waitress was still standing above me, paying attention, but I sensed that she was becoming uncomfortable, so I picked up my fork and looked at my food to give her an excuse to exit.

She was quiet for a moment longer, like she was contemplating what I had just said, but it didn't last long. Before she turned to weave her way in and out of the tables back across the room, she said, "Enjoy your food. I hope you figure things out."

9
Veil of Guilt

*In the dead of the night, in the still and the quiet I slip
away like a bird in flight. Back to those hills, the place I
call home.*

—"West Virginia, My Home Sweet Home," first official state song,
by Colonel Julian G. Hearne Jr., 1947

It was an especially long drive home from Athens; the depth of the
guilt I was experiencing made me feel like I was in high school again
at a cotillion dance waltzing with a boy, but wishing instead I was with
my best friend across the room. I also fell in love with her on a bicycle—
mine was a Schwinn and hers was a Raleigh—but I never confessed my
love to her. I was too young and naive; I saw no other way to be. But
now I was so tired of living in the fog. I wasn't sixteen anymore.

I was scared to go home. I felt there was no way to hide my decep-
tion—that somehow Sam would see through me and understand
exactly what had happened while I was in Athens. My heart raced
with the speed of the fields and mountains passing by my windows
the entire ride home. I've never been a good liar.

From: Carrie
To: Charlie
Subject: Oops/frustration

Charlie,
    Oops . . . I sent an e-mail back to you. Sorry.

On another note, Nelson came home from school looking very frustrated. He went in his room and hasn't been out all afternoon or evening. I knocked, but he said that he was fine and to leave him alone. I'm trying to give him space. I know when Quinn is angry because he wears it on his sleeve.

There is a balance to do what is right and wrong with children each and every day. Hope I'm not tipping the scale too much either way.
Carrie

From: Charlie
To: Carrie
Subject: Oops/frustration

Carrie,

I do the same thing—send e-mails back to you.

I worry that Nelson never gets angry and hope he is not keeping everything inside. Everyone needs some way to work off frustration. Keep an eye on him, and I think you will figure out when to step in.

I have never experienced Quinn's angry fits. I guess I really don't know him that well yet.
Charlie

I couldn't help but think the whole way home about the "oops" I had committed with Ryann. There was no turning around. Why does real—totally real—love make us feel like we can fly? Who would give us that feeling and in another breath take it away? I finally acted on something that I'd been hiding for years, and I had been awakened to a new reality—but I had a pretty good notion that when I walked through the door and saw Sam and the boys, I would keep hiding behind the label I was trying to live up to. The only thing harder than remaining trapped in the status quo was admitting to myself, to my family, and to everyone else that I wasn't who I seemed to be.

As I pulled into the driveway, the gravel rubbed together extra loud, causing a sharp echo in my ears. I turned the car off and sat for a moment, hoping no one inside had heard. The shadow of the boys' bunk bed and Sam moving around their room sent a wave of fear through my body that froze me still as the night air outside. How could I ever walk away and change this family forever?

I was consumed with thoughts of backing up and running away, without a clue as to where I would go if I did. Ryann was just a few short blocks away with her family, but we had not spoken since she left my hotel room in Athens. I felt so alone; the memory of her breathing beside me back in Athens resonated in my mind. I rested my forehead on the steering wheel and settled into my fog for at least twenty minutes. Shortly after the boys' light dimmed, I mustered up enough courage to go inside.

As I was reaching for the door it, suddenly opened and Sam was standing just inside staring at me. He looked manic, scary—at least, that's what my paranoia was telling me to see—and I flinched with an electric fear that sent a quick sweat from my spine clear down to my toes. *This must be what a falling star feels when it's dropping from the sky.* I wobbled on my feet a little and looked at Sam with my mouth half open.

My bag slipped off my shoulder to the floor, and Sam reached for the strap. "How long have you been here?" he asked.

"I just got here . . . why?"

"Oh, because I thought I heard you come in a while ago."

I became angry and snatched my bag back from him, stumbling in my haste. "It hasn't been that long; I was just getting my things together." I stepped sideways in through the door, avoiding the kiss he was trying to give me. I sat my bag on the couch just inside and looked half way down to the floor to avoid eye contact and said, "I'm tired, I need to go back out and get my bike off the rack."

"I'll get your bike." He walked abruptly out the door.

The air inside had a familiar aroma, a comfortable smell, but I could still smell Ryann radiating from my clothes. I looked up at the ceiling and closed my exhausted eyes for a moment while I listened to the boys talking to one another above me. I had this overwhelming feeling that this moment was a beginning and also an end for me.

The door closing behind me startled me. I looked back to see Sam standing just inside with my bike in his hands. I smiled a little smile at him, trying to hide my sadness I was wearing like a cloak over my body.

"Thank you."

He walked by me and put my bike in its corner by the dining room table. I realized my bike and I had a comfortable spot here in this home, and to move either one would upset the familiar not only for me but for so many others who ran deep in my heart.

Sam came back and sat down on the couch. "You're welcome. How was your trip? I bet it was fun."

I kept standing; I was afraid if I retreated to a chair, I would remorsefully hide behind crossed arms and begin rocking. Pacing back and forth with my hands clasped behind my back was better for me at the moment.

"The countryside is beautiful around Athens—I saw a part we didn't get to see much of when you were considering the residency program there."

"Did you get much riding in? I know how much you like to ride with Ryann."

"We rode thirty-four miles and ate at the Grit."

He looked up at me. "Yum. I remember it there—good food."

Trying to avoid his stare, I looked beyond him out the window. "It was pretty much the same, really yummy."

"What did you get to eat?" he asked.

"I had the hummus platter with falafel and tabouleh. Ryann got the special, but I can't remember what it was."

I must have appeared nervous, pacing restlessly in front of him and squeezing my palms together, because he asked, "Do you need to go to the bathroom or something?"

I jumped all over the opportunity to exit the most uncomfortable juncture in my life thus far. I whimpered a pathetic "yes" and turned to run upstairs, like a child. Each wooden step echoed louder in my ears as I tried to get to the top and out of Sam's sight.

I ducked for cover behind the bathroom door and began pacing at breakneck speed on the tile floor. I was so caught up with hiding what I had done in Athens that I hadn't even bothered to ask Sam about his weekend with the boys. How had I become so selfish?

My breathing became extra heavy, and I knew if I didn't get control of myself, I was going to lose my cookies and have a nervous breakdown right there. I went straight for the mirror and strained once again to try to figure out who this person staring back at me was. "You're staying in there," I told myself through gritted teeth. "*This* is your family—not Ryann." Then I pointed directly at my reflection and said, "That's it—don't come out again!"

How much can a person speak to herself before a psychological evaluation is needed? I was beginning to see a padded room and a psychiatrist on my horizon.

I turned away from the mirror and undressed to take a shower, hoping to wash the guilt and gayness away for good. My gosh . . . I'd taken thousands of showers that I hoped would wash away my homosexuality, but here I was again. How hard must you scrub in order to erase the skin you live in every day? It didn't seem to be working. I don't know why I thought tonight would be any different.

I had accidentally left the door open, and Sam came in as I was stepping out of the shower and onto the tile floor. I felt the striking cold go from my feet directly up to my heart. I wished I had remembered to put down a bath mat.

"Did the Grit look the same?" he asked, handing me a towel.

There was a difficult pause, and my paranoia peeked its way out again. "What's with all the questions about the Grit?"

He looked right in my eyes and let out a sigh. "I don't know. I was just wondering."

I took the towel from his hand and answered firmly, "Yes, it looks the same." Then I grabbed his hand and pulled him to me. I kissed him with all the disgrace I had bottled up inside. I was so confused that I didn't want to speak a word; I just wanted to rectify the situation by loving Sam the way I had loved Ryann just two days before. If I took away the love I gave her and gave it to him, I thought, that would make it all better, right?

Sam stumbled backward and caught his balance on the sink. "Whoa, what has gotten into you? You're all wet!"

"I missed you." I leaned my wet, quivering body back into his, and as he was getting ready to speak again, I kissed the words right out of him. I was so afraid of him asking a question that I would have to answer dishonestly. It was better if I just kept both of us quiet. I felt the comfort of my home—the home that I had just considered leaving—rush through me as he wrapped his arms around me and returned the kiss. My mind was tangled with anger and remorse, and I was drowning in it. There was no way I was going to make a rational decision anytime soon.

I dropped my towel to the floor and let Sam lead me naked through the hall to our bedroom. I wished there was a way I could expose what was going on inside me as easily as I was revealing my nude body to him. But the physical act was much easier than my mental state at the moment, so I joined him in our bed. He laid me gently down and sat on the edge as he removed his clothes. I was hoping for a reprieve from what I thought was going to happen next: a false love. He lay down beside me and his light sandpaper cheek touched mine.

"I love you," he whispered. His voice was full of suspicion, and it had a questioning quality to it, as if he knew I was already gone.

A tear was rolling from the corner of my eye, and I was thankful for the darkness. I turned away and looked at the moon and the stars shining outside. My mind was frantic, like a spring thunderstorm. Sam was hovering above me and kissing my cheek, waiting on an answer. His warm breath aggravated me and sent chills through my body, but I put my arms around him and answered like a robot, "I love you too."

In the darkness we moved over the familiar maps of our bodies, as we had done for so many years. Only this time, I was mostly just exasperated. My hands, arms, and legs still held lingering fatigue from Athens, and I was simultaneously angry at myself for being capable of such fraud and upset at the world because I felt like a prisoner in my own home. But most of all, I felt scared—scared beyond my capacity of emotions that I might lose my family.

I took all that bottled-up, fearful anger and tried as best I could to turn it into love that evening, but it was no use. And the anger and fear must have been seeping out of me, because Sam recognized that something was off. He brought his breath back to my ear and said, "You're everywhere but here."

My mind was on overload. I just wanted to curl up in a fetal position and turn that one tear into a thousand. I said the only thing that came to mind: "I'm sorry. I'm just tired from the trip."

He ended things quickly and turned away from me.

How can I possibly keep up this facade for a lifetime? The only way would be to leave West Virginia so I wouldn't see Ryann anymore. Luckily, that was probably going to happen: Sam was about to finish his residency, and we had already been talking about relocating to North Carolina, where we had started our life together. My mind fast-forwarded to what I would do: go back in the closet, stick by my family, move away, forget Ryann, and be straight forever. I was sure it would play out perfectly. With all the other moves, I had gone kicking and screaming; this time I was going to push for it to happen as quickly as possible.

I reached for Sam's shoulder and pulled him toward me. He resisted. The fear of desertion was filling up both sides of our lonely bed.

"Did you hear from the hospital in North Carolina?" I asked.

He didn't look at me, and I could tell he was in a distant place from the hollow sound in his voice. I wondered if that faraway place had frightened visions of life without me. That was what I was trying to fathom at the moment: life without him.

"They called on Friday and I should know something by Monday," he said.

"Are they going to help financially to set up your practice?"

"They may help up front, but I'll have to pay it back over a period of time."

I turned away from him and covered my cold body with the blankets. "Well, how soon do you think we will be able to move if it works out?"

"Probably around November or October if everything goes as planned."

"I don't want to move the boys in the middle of school again," I said. "If you decide to make the move, I'll go early and register the boys in school there."

He pulled the covers with a slight but forceful roll, as if he was angry, and said, "There's too much to discuss tonight. We can talk about it later."

"All right, then—tomorrow we need to try to figure this out." I was happy the conversation ended.

We fell asleep facing opposite directions. The bitter gap between us was palpable all night, as we both avoided each other's slightest touch.

———

At the first sight of light creeping through the shades, after a night of tossing and turning, I pulled my disgraceful body out of bed and snuck downstairs to make coffee. The boys would go to school in a few hours, and Sam would go to work. I stood in the kitchen staring at the dripping coffee and waiting impatiently for that time to come. I wanted to be alone in our home so I could filter through my thoughts about my tryst with Ryann in Georgia, my home in West Virginia, and my move to North Carolina.

The coffee noise and aroma must have woken Sam, because as I turned to get a mug out of the cabinet I saw him leaning in the doorway staring at me. It startled me a bit and my hand froze in midair. He was fully dressed, with his briefcase in his hand, and I wondered how long he had been standing there.

"It's six o'clock. Are you going to work right now?"

He looked tired; dark circles hung under his eyes. I felt that tired, and I wondered if my eyes looked that way too. Realizing my hand was still hesitantly floating in the air along with the dust motes illuminated by the sunlight peering through the window, I quickly reached for the mug.

"Yes, I thought I would go in early to catch up on some dictation."

I think he wanted to get out of my sight just as much as I wanted him out of my sight. We were both feeling the growing distance between us, though neither one of us wanted to acknowledge it.

I looked back at the coffee as if it was going to bail me out in some way. Wanting to avoid eye contact, I shot a quick, nervous glance back at him before saying, "Well . . . I hope you have a good day." With that, I returned my stare to the coffeemaker.

He didn't reply, and I heard his footsteps begin to fade away toward the front door. A gulp of air, full of despair, came out when I heard the front door shut with a bang that boomed through the whole house.

This was what I'd wanted—time for processing—but now I was scared to be alone. The walls were echoing silence off the wood floors. The last bit of steam hissed out of the coffeemaker, and I felt completely deserted. Piece by piece, Sam was figuring out that I was slipping away, and I hadn't heard from Ryann since we left Athens. It was eating away at me inside; I so wanted to talk to her, be with her, hold her.

I got a cup of coffee and went into the dining room to sit by myself. The chair was cold, but I wondered if my heart was colder. It sure felt like it was right then. How strange it is when the mind and heart play opposing games with each other and make love a frightening mystery that leaves you feeling naked and alone, in the middle of a blizzard.

Just as I was beginning my pity party, slumped over my coffee, the phone rang. I jumped up and knocked the chair to the floor; it hit the ground with a solid bang as I slid on my socks over to the phone to view the caller ID.

It was Ryann; so much for being alone. A hot flash blinded my sight and sent my body into a childish panic. I reached for the phone but stopped midway there. *Should I pick it up, or should I not?*

My contemplation was interrupted by a little voice behind me. "Hey, Mommy."

I turned around and looked first at Quinn, who was standing behind me, rubbing his eyes with his fists, then at the ringing phone, and then back at him again. I opened my arms and motioned for him to come toward me. "Hey there, sweetie. Come here."

His itty-bitty, naked feet pattered on the floor as he walked over to me. Nelson appeared just as I picked Quinn up and hugged him with all my might. The ringing phone faded away as I breathed his sweet, innocent smell deep into my lungs. I made my mind up then and there to stay in my hidden life—after all, I was the one who had created it.

Part Two
North Carolina

Esse quam videri.
"To be, rather than to seem."

10
Good-bye

Oh, the West Virginia Hills! I must bid you now adieu.
In my home beyond the mountains, I shall ever dream
of you.

—"West Virginia Hills," West Virginia state song,
words by Ellen Rudell King

The boys and I moved to North Carolina just a little over a month
after I came back from the state where red clay is abundant and
the song "Georgia on My Mind" had sung a ballad of unfaithfulness
in my heart. The Ray Charles version had a way of throwing me into a
tornado of screaming emotions.

From: Carrie
To: Charlie
Subject: Quiche

Charlie,
*   I'm glad I was able to come over and share quiche, salad,*
and flowers with you and Anne. You have done so much for me,
and Anne is so kind for letting my family share you. I enjoyed
visiting; wish it could have been longer.
*   Sometimes I miss the small, quaint towns in West Virginia,*
but then I remember all my city friends who have made me feel

at home and taught me how to live life to its fullest among the hustle and bustle, and I don't want to go back.
Carrie

From: *Charlie*
To: *Carrie*
Subject: *Quiche*

Carrie,

You are just a country girl thrown by circumstances in the bustling "metropolis" of Asheville. You won't believe this, but I think you would get bored back there. However, it is a terrific retreat from your crazy life every now and then.

You really brightened both Anne and my lives with your gift of food, beauty, and time. The salad was delicious, blueberries so fresh and juicy, granola was wonderful, and the goat cheese was just the right topping. The quiche was just perfectly done and really hit the spot. They both were so good, we made two meals of it and just finished the second one for our lunch. What wonderful, thoughtful gifts.
Charlie

My sons and I left West Virginia a month before school started to avoid another transfer between schools. Sam was to come six months later when he finished his residency.

The day of our move, the boys had gone outside to play on their swing set, yelling, "We have to say good-bye to our swings!" They were excited about the adventure we were about to undertake. *A beginning is always exciting—until the newness wears off and you're right back where you started, living with yourself once again, just in a new place and time*, I thought, but I was glad they were happy about the move. I was thankful as well that they had each other. It built a strong bond between them that only they could understand.

Sam said his good-byes to us early, before leaving for work, and the car was loaded to its maximum loading potential. I crammed stuff in every open space available inside of the car and in the soft black luggage rack tied on top. It looked like it might bust at the seams and explode, dropping all our prized possessions, as soon as we started heading south on Interstate 77 to North Carolina. On top of everything else, there were four bikes hanging from a rack on the back of the car: my mountain bike, my road bike, and the boys' bikes. I knew there was good riding in Asheville and I was going to be prepared.

Ryann and I had only seen each other twice since our affair, and both times it was quick and awkward. We both knew it was only torture to be together, so we had chosen to stay away from one another. But now, as I came to the bottom of the stairs inside the house carrying one last bag, I spotted her on the front porch, peering over the railing at my car. My heart sank for a moment as I opened the door, but then I drummed up some false courage and put on my game face. *No shaking allowed*, I told myself.

I pushed the door open. "Hey . . . how . . . are you?" *So much for my voice not shaking.*

Ryann jumped back slightly and turned quickly, as if I had caught her in the middle of doing something wrong. She looked happy to see me, but there was a bruised weariness behind her smile. Her reply was as scrambled as her face looked. "I'm just . . . oh, I'm good. I . . . I've really missed you."

"I've missed you too," I said. My voice was still quavering a little. I looked out beyond her and held my bag up in the air. "I have to take this last bag to the car. Do you mind waiting inside?"

"No, sure," she said hastily.

I could feel our lie, buried in sorrow, radiating between us as we edged past each other, heading in opposite directions.

I bolted the rest of the way to the car and shoved the bag in between the boys' seats, adding to the wall of luggage that would be separating them as we drove, then sprinted back to the house. When I walked inside, Ryann was on the couch with a card in her hand. The unrelenting fascination going on between us was still there, so much so that I was fighting to keep the attraction under control. It felt like a hot, humid summer night had taken over the room.

"Hey, I have a card for you too. Let me go get it." Everything went quiet; the only sound in the room came from my heavy steps across the wood floor.

I came back holding my card close to my heart and again said, "I'm going to miss you."

"I'm going to miss you too," Ryann echoed.

It was best to stop there, at "I'll miss yous," and exchange cards, which inside cried love for our friendship, for meeting one another, and for the future we might have had that would never come to pass. I was an expert at good-byes.

I motioned for Ryann to come over and give me a hug. As we embraced, I felt her shaking, and I wondered if she could feel me shaking, too. I desperately wanted to answer the passion that was beyond the embrace of a jittery hug. But I also wanted to make my family happy, so I pushed away, and so did she. She wasn't planning on leaving her family, either. We both dropped our hands down by our sides and looked away, and then she moved over to the door and peered out at my car. "You're really loaded down. Hope your trip is safe. Will you give me a call when you get situated?"

"Yes, I'll call," I said, but knew inside that I wouldn't; it would only perpetuate the inevitable.

She would tell me later that the sight of my loaded car, as well as the first time she went to pick up Alex from elementary school and realized I wasn't there, waiting on my own boys, hurt her enough to bring tears to her eyes. But she did her best to get through it, because she had to, just as I did.

After we hugged good-bye, Ryann let me walk her to the car, unlike our parting in Georgia—I guess maybe because she knew this parting was going to be permanent. After all, a combination of approximately two hundred miles of mountains, valleys, and corridors would soon be separating us. No longer would I be up all night, contemplating and conjuring up ways I could sneak the few short blocks to be with her.

We hugged one more time before she got in her car, and after pushing the door closed behind her to make sure we had a boundary separating us, I kissed two of my fingers and gently touched her cheek through the open window. She smiled sternly and put both hands on the steering wheel, and I watched as she once again disappeared down the road. My heart felt heavy, but it was much easier to push my tears away now that I had set my mind to doing what I thought was right.

I walked around the back to the boys and what was left of my short-season garden, which was still full of dusty dirt and rocks. I hadn't had time to make the soil dark and rich, or to grow anything beyond some lettuce and corn to feed my family. I'd always dreamed I would be like my grandmother, who spent summer after summer keeping watch over a big silver pot full of mason jars crying steam. By the end of each summer, her cabinets were full of love and nourishment in a rainbow of colors, and I knew I wanted food like that—but I'd never had enough time to dabble in it because life was so full of transition for us.

"Hey guys, we have to get on the road. Let's go say good-bye to Clara and Carlton."

The boys had collected substitute grandparents with each move. Clara and Carlton were the best ones yet, with only two houses separating us. The boys usually attracted couples who didn't have grandkids of their own. In their own way, they were all helping one another pass the lonely times during the week between school and church. Since we'd lived in this house, the boys had traveled the sidewalk to Clara and Carlton's house almost every day to play hide and seek, miniature golf, or cards, or just to sit and gab on the front porch, drinking lemonade and pumping their legs high on the porch swing.

Clara taught Quinn how to play his first game of fifty-two-card pickup in her sunroom. I was sitting by when she threw them in the air. The cards caught the sun's reflection as they drifted down to the carpet. I tried to hide my giggle, but it was no use; along with Clara,

I succumbed to heavy laughter. I didn't think I would ever hear the end of that one—Quinn was so mad he had fallen for it. "Why didn't you tell me?" he would say. Ever since, every now and then when we were visiting, Clara would look right at Quinn with a sly smile and a twinkle in her eyes and say, "You wanna play fifty-two-card pickup?"

Carter could always be found in his brown chair in the corner of the room with an enduring smile on his face. He said little, but what he did say to the boys was powerful—things like, "You two are going places. I can feel it in my bones." Clara, meanwhile, liked to say to me, "Carrie, you have static in your attic." She usually said it when she saw me goofing off with the boys. I guessed that she didn't know how serious or true her words actually were.

The boys came down off the swings quickly, without putting up a fight—unusual for them. As I walked behind them on the sidewalk, I noticed that their shoulders were slumped over a little—in anticipation of the farewell speech we were about to impose on our favorite neighbors, I supposed.

Clara and Carter came right to the door when we rang the bell, as if they were waiting on us. They were both small in stature, with gray hair and fragile-looking bodies—as the case usually is when you have eighty years of moving up and down and all around behind you. Clara was one of those people who had a permanent smile; in the past it had seemed like nothing could ever break it, but today it was smaller than I'd ever seen it.

She put both arms up and out to her side, inviting the boys to come and fill the space in under them. They skipped right over to her and stacked both arms on each other around her waist and began squeezing. It was hard to tell who was hugging harder. Carter stepped from behind her and waited for his hug. Both boys were trying to hide their crying by tucking their heads into her pillowy sides, as if it was an embarrassment for little boys to cry.

"So I guess this is good-bye," Clara said, looking at me.

I couldn't say anything; my mind was exhausted from all these farewells. I tried to muster up a smile, but it was no use—my cheeks blew up with air and my lips turned down. I joined the group hug, and lo and behold if Carter didn't join in and squeeze the hardest. We stood there in a huddle and rocked round and round for what seemed to be forever until Clara broke the silence: "Do you think you can keep your static under control, Carrie?"

We all let go and coughed out chuckles mixed with sobs.

"I'm going to try . . . I promise," I said.

When we had wiped away our tears, I said, "Well, I guess we better head out; we can't turn back the hands of time."

"We're going to miss our two favorite boys," Carter said.

Both boys replied, "We're going to miss you, too."

"Ditto," I added, before grabbing the boys' hands and pulling them with me down the sidewalk. We all looked back after a few steps, and there were Clara and Carter, standing with their arms about one another and waving. The boys waved back, and I could feel them lightly tugging backward on my hands. It took all the emotional strength I had left to hold tight and lead them to the car.

When I had the boys packed in, I made sure I didn't look back again. We were all in tears for the first hour. I tried to console them with talk of all the new places we would visit and explore when we arrived in North Carolina, but deep inside I was having trouble believing that this move was best for all of us. I was especially afraid to leave my closeted life with Sam. It was all I knew; even if it was dysfunctional, I felt the most secure there, and so did the boys. If I left, where would I go?

—

It took three and a half hours to get to our rental home, which was huge compared with what we had left back in West Virginia. It was intimidating, except for the fact that it was up on top of a mountain that overlooked a valley full of cows, which made me feel like we were back home in West Virginia. I could lie to myself and the boys, saying, "Don't worry. We're still in the Appalachian Mountains."

As soon as we'd moved all our things inside, I called Sam, knowing he would still be at work. *Hallelujah*, I thought when I heard the *beep* of his voice mail on the other end of the line.

"Hey," I said. "We made it safe and sound . . . there is no need to call us back. I'm going to be busy unpacking and cooking dinner." Then I abruptly hung up in case he was anywhere in the vicinity of his phone. I didn't want to give him a chance to pick it up.

My stomach churned when I thought of Ryann's last words: to call her when I got situated. I made a quick decision not to do it. What was the point? So we could tell one another that good-bye meant good-bye? Or so we could cry again? *How many times is a heart able to break before it's irreparable?* I wondered. I needed all the strength I could wrangle up to hide the relentless guilt that had overtaken my body and mind.

I turned my attention to the house. Funny how space works—we had been so crowded in the car, but the house felt extra empty even with all our things in there. The boys and I found a green plastic table outside and turned it on its side and rolled it into the kitchen to go with our canvas fold-up chairs I'd brought along.

When we sat down to eat our dinner, I realized that my chest barely reached the top of the table, while the boys' eyes just peeked over the top. I ducked down so my eyes were level with theirs, stuck my tongue out, and peered side to side with only my eyeballs. We all laughed out loud. This was the routine of new places: laugh first, cry later.

"We can go explore tomorrow," I said.

"Like explore what?" Quinn said. "I want to go back."

"I don't like it here," Nelson agreed. "Can we please go back?"

I'd had a feeling this was coming—it was just here sooner than I'd thought it would be. "Let's wake up tomorrow with a fresh start and see what North Carolina has to offer."

"No," Quinn said forcefully.

Nelson added, "I don't like it here."

"How can you feel that way when you haven't even given it a chance?" I asked.

"Because I just know," Quinn said. "All my friends are back in West Virginia. . . . Please, Mom—I want to go back."

"Guys, let's just sleep on it tonight," I said, knowing there was no way to dissuade them from their stubborn moods. "Tomorrow when we get up, we'll go explore new things."

Ha! Who did I think I was fooling? I wanted to go back just as much—maybe more—than they did. I kept smothering those deranged thoughts, but they were visiting my mind more and more, like little psychotic tics. I couldn't seem to keep them under control.

We were all exhausted from our trip south, so as soon as dinner was over, I got the boys in the bath and to bed right away, then went to my own room and crawled in bed. For a while, all I could hear was our breathing, which was not enough to take away the silent stillness. I was feeling as hollow inside as that big old house. Then the boys started in again:

"I'm scared here," Nelson said. "Can we please go back?"

"No, we're staying here," I said. "This is where Dad is going to be working, and we can't change that now."

Before I could say anything more, Quinn interrupted me from his room: "Please, Mom, please, we want to go back." His sad voice hurt my soul.

They both started to whimper, but the sound quickly became much louder than a whimper because their cries rebounded off the rubber of their air mattresses and around the wooden floors and walls of their empty rooms. There was nothing to soften the disturbing noise.

"I'm moving into the room with Nelson," Quinn finally moaned out, his words barely comprehensible between his tearful sobs. Instantly I heard some shuffling around, and then the sound of his mattress being dragged and his feet pitter-pattering from one room to the other. I thought about how that mattress must be three times his size, but I didn't get up, and he managed it all by himself. The boys whispered and cried themselves to sleep in that vacant house, and I did too—the only difference was that my heartache was not innocent, and I didn't let my tears or sobs ring out into the air. The boys shared their sorrow with each other, but I shared mine only with the pillows I was hugging tight.

—

The next day we visited a really interesting general store that sold all kinds of old-fashioned things, and I bought the boys a few goodies and then took them outside to people-watch, an art I learned during my summer visits with my grandparents in Kentucky. Asheville's diverse array of residents and visitors made it an ideal place to observe people and imagine trading places with them. On this day, all of the imaginary homes I went to were full of happy people and welcoming arms. My guess was that the boys were imagining being in happy homes also, because they were smiling a lot and seemed to have forgotten about their tears from the night before.

For the next few weeks we explored coffee shops, parks, science centers, and art museums. Within the week I joined the YMCA so I could go to spinning class and hopefully meet some fellow cyclists, and also to give the boys an opportunity to get to know the local kids outside of school.

After my third spinning class I worked up the nerve to approach the outgoing blonde on the spin bike beside me. There was a deep hankering burning inside to find out about road rides in the area; I had been away from black pavement much too long. The class ended and we were all cleaning our bikes.

"Do you ride outside, on the road . . . or in the woods?" I asked the woman, as I reached for the cleaning solution she was finishing up with.

"No, I don't do either—just spinning classes. What about you?"

I gave her a short, slight smile, feeling a bit sad she was not a cyclist. "I ride outside—do you know anybody who does? I've just moved to the area, and I'm trying to find some people to ride with."

She looked at my legs and replied, "You die-hard cyclists have this breed of legs that stands out among athletes—a little on the top-heavy side. My neighbor Sara goes riding all the time with this tall, older guy named Charlie. I think you'd love both of them."

I slapped the sides of both my thighs in the vicinity of what I thought she meant was the "top-heavy" area. "Really? Thanks, but it's just genetics. Do you think I could meet your neighbor? I need someone to help familiarize me with safe roads to ride on around here. I would feel much safer if I'm riding with someone. At least until I can make my own routes without getting lost."

"Yeah, I'm sure she would love to talk to you. She's particularly talented when it comes to social skills. She talks a lot, so beware if you're in a hurry. Hold on a minute while I get a piece of paper and write her number down for you."

"Thanks a bunch; that would be great."

As the woman walked over to the table in the corner of the room, my eyes trailed right behind her and I thought to myself how beautifully in shape she was. *What does she see in my legs that she thinks she doesn't have?* I wondered. I stopped thinking about her beauty and followed her over to the table.

While she was writing on the paper, she said, "Her name is Sara, and she's so much fun—like the kid in the neighborhood who everyone wants to play with. Do you remember those kids growing up?"

"Yes, for sure—don't we all?"

She handed me the number and I smiled as I took it. "Thanks! Would you please let her know that a fellow cyclist who has just moved here will most likely be calling her this week?"

"Sure, but what's your name, so I can let her know?"

"Silly me—how could I forget something so important?" I blushed. "I'm Carrie Highley. I just moved here from West Virginia with my husband and two sons."

11
High-Speed Wobble

Our hearts understand one another.

—Dolly Madison, born May 20, 1768, Greensboro, North Carolina

I connected with Sara and Charlie at the same time my connection with Sam was becoming vastly lost. All my free moments were spent with them learning the back roads of Buncombe, Henderson, and Madison Counties. The most memorable ride was one the three of us did with another group of riders to the top of Mount Pisgah via the Blue Ridge Parkway. We climbed from approximately two thousand feet of elevation to almost five thousand feet to get to our midway destination, the Pisgah Inn. Once there, we enjoyed lunch and a panoramic view of the area's "blue" mountains.

When I started out on the nineteen-mile climb to the top, I knew it was going to be difficult, so I immediately started looking for someone to draft behind. Drafting works something like this: the front rider blocks the headwind, creating wind turbulence behind them, and in turn this generates little vortexes that pull the rider behind them along after them. Proper etiquette is to take turns being the head rider, but I managed to meander my way around the other riders to the back of Charlie's tire, and we never switched positions; he pulled me all the way to the top of Mount Pisgah. At the time, I had no idea his drafting support on a bicycle would carry over to drafting sustenance off the bike as well.

From: Carrie
To: Charlie
Subject: Friend

Charlie,

You are a wonderful friend. I want to say this in all serious-ness: the last words I speak every night are "thank you." Not only for you and all my friends and family, but for all the mag-nificent gifts I have been given in my life. I mean this with all my heart. I wouldn't change all the crazy, hard moments for anything in the world.

Route 276 has brand-new pavement, I would love to go downhill on it to see how fast I can go. Are you up to it when you get back? I wish there were two weekends in a workweek. I think my motto will be "Never, never, never grow up—that makes you old. Life is a ride!"

I wanted you to know I went to South College last week and applied to the physical therapy assistant program. I just have to go in and interview next week. I think it will tie in well with my bachelor's degree, and hopefully if Sam and I get a divorce I will be able to support myself and the boys.

Have a safe and wonderful trip on your vacation out West with Anne. I hope you get this before you leave. Just wanted you to know you're gonna be missed! Also hoping I'm as moti-vated without your motivation on the rides next week.
Carrie

To: Carrie
From: Charlie
Subject: Friend

Carrie,

You are a wonderful friend too who brings so much sunshine

*in my life. When I get back we will go for a ride on 276. Just
keep moving forward, and you will find solutions.*

*Speaking of old, remember, you have to take me out to lunch
when I'm in the old folks' home.*

*I'm glad you decided to sign up for the program at South
College. I think you are right and that it will be a good cushion
to have in case of divorce.*
Charlie

About a year into my friendship with Charlie, we had grown
extremely close, and I found myself constantly digging around in my
soul for the courage to tell him what I so desperately needed to disclose. I felt like a downright dirty liar, keeping such pertinent information from the foundation of our friendship; I don't know who I
thought I was fooling.

Finally, one day, as Charlie and I were riding up North Mills River
Road in the cool damp air, it began to yelp up in my throat and I had
to get it out so I could breathe again. My face became red with fire and,
spinning my pedals at record speed, I emitted a squeaky, fearful sigh
and said, "Charlie . . . have you heard any rumors about me?"

I guess I must have sounded extremely worried when I asked
because he answered back quickly and firmly: "No. Is there something
wrong, Carrie? Are you sick?"

I looked down at his pedals and watched them go round and round
for a few moments, feeling the numbness of my ears and toes in the
wind. My mind became circles of thoughts. *How do I say it? Is he going
to pass judgment? Will he still be my friend, and what will he think?*

"Umm . . . oh, I was just wondering." I was sure he could hear the
anxiety making my voice tremble. "I'm sorry," I blurted out, "my teeth
are not chattering from the cold; I have something really important
to tell you, but I'm scared. That would explain why my mouth sounds
like a babbling brook."

Charlie shifted himself on his bike and turned his neck to look
back at me. His glance was as intense as he could possibly make it

while moving quickly ahead on his bicycle. He spoke over the passing wind. "I hope I have never given you any reason to be afraid to tell me the truth."

I pushed my pedals hard to get up next to him. "No, you have always understood and been open to hear anything I say, but this . . . it could change your every thought about me. What if I'm really not the Carrie you thought I was . . . like, I have a secret I've never shared with anyone? It could make you want to ride away from me and never come back." I swallowed. "But I hope it won't!"

He craned his neck to look over at me and cleared his throat. "Nothing could do that," he said with fierce certainty in his voice. "I've invested too much time in you."

My legs were still pedaling extra fast, and the mechanical sound of the chain going around and around was echoing in my ears and interrupting my thoughts—strange, because that sound usually had a way of organizing my thoughts. But right now I was on fire inside with how to tell one of my best friends in the world the whole truth and nothing but the truth. And it was not an easy truth; it had a way of stirring up emotions higher even than Snake Mountain, the hardest climb I experienced on my bicycle after I moved to North Carolina. Each time I thought about disclosing my secret, my body had exploded into menopausal hot flashes and foggy-brain syndrome, and this time was no exception.

When love crystallizes between two people and the boundaries between them dissolve, things happen that you know full well shouldn't happen—like losing control and erasing every aspect of what you thought your life was. How could I explain to Charlie that this is what had happened to me three years earlier in West Virginia?

Those multitudes of thoughts circled my mind and bounced back and forth with fear, yet slowly but surely, they came out in that September wind in the form of just three little words: "Charlie . . . I'm gay."

The wind had picked up and was so strong in that moment that it was concealing Charlie's words. He was replying, but I couldn't hear what he was saying, and in my anxiety I spent a couple of miles assuming the worst. But then, finally, I began to comprehend his words.

"It's okay," he was saying. "Carrie, you are who you are, and to love someone is a wonderful thing."

He offered no judgment on the idea of loving the same sex in his reply—just true, unconditional support. This seemed to come naturally to Charlie. I took a second to bask in this moment—something I had been longing to feel for so many years. The clamorous wind I had created in my mind subsided, and courage began to pump through my legs in cranking revolutions on my bicycle as I rode beside my most amazing buddy. *One friend down*, I thought. I tried not to dwell on how many more I had to go—and let's not forget about my conservative family, who would quite possibly think the "closet" would be the best place for me.

Revealing my hidden self for the first time catapulted me into uncontrollable trembling inside and out. My body was shaking all over—I felt like I did when I experienced my first high-speed wobble coming down Roan Mountain shortly after I moved to Asheville.

—

That event took place when a couple of friends and I were out riding north of Asheville one warm, sunny day. As I crested the top of the mountain on my seventeen-pound bike, visions of the Tour de France boys in my mind, I yelled out, "I'm going to beat all of you to the bottom!"

Looking back over my shoulder, I saw that my friends were just a few feet behind me, and they all jumped to stand on their pedals in acceptance of my challenge.

A few "yeah, rights" and a distinct "I don't think so!" echoed like a cracking whip in the air behind me—just what I needed to hear to get my competitive nature stirred up—and I crouched down tight over the top of my bicycle like a little roly-poly bug and began pumping my legs, accelerating my odometer from thirty to forty within seconds.

As the shadow of one of my contenders appeared in my peripheral vision, I yelled over my shoulder, "Ha . . . we'll see about that, won't we!" and pushed my pedals harder and faster, reaching forty-eight. Halfway down the hill I was still in front and already contemplating how the race would end: with me waving my hands high in the warm breeze, celebrating my victory.

I was enjoying my fastest speed ever, with the summer wind whistling through my helmet, when my tire rolled over a pebble. It was tinier than a green pea, but it was just big and hard enough to send my wheel into an uncontrollable wobble over the black pavement.

The bandits chasing me blasted by with little effort, shouting, "We won! See you at the bottom!" They didn't even notice I was in a desperate way.

My bike was vibrating out of control, and I was sure my life was about to end in a crash along the road. But I wasn't ready for that; I still had a very important secret to share with my loved ones—especially my boys. Somehow, even in this dizzy, trembling fog that had overtaken me as soon as I'd lost control of my bike, I had enough sense to hug my top tube with my thighs while intermittently squeezing my brakes, and I was able to pull myself out of my first (and, I hoped, last) high speed wobble.

By confiding in Charlie, I had just sent the very essence of my soul into frantic emotional and mental vibrations, but I was lacking something important: there was no top tube in my life to help me hug my way to safety. Talking with Charlie had made me feel better, but I still had no idea how I was going to tell the rest of my loved ones about the demon crying out from within me.

12
Acceptance

It's never too late to have a happy childhood.

—Tom Robbins, born July 22, 1932, Blowing Rock, North Carolina

The raw moments of the day drifted into my sleep as I thought of what my e-mail in the morning would say to Charlie. His response the day before made me realize that there would be people who would accept me for all I was, and that the ones who didn't I would have to learn to let go of and dismiss from my life. I wondered if he had told his wife, Anne, about my confession, and if it would calm any worries she might have about our devoted friendship.

From: Carrie
To: Charlie
Subject: Thanks for listening

Charlie,

That was really difficult for me to tell you, but you are such an important person in my life that I had to be honest with you. Sorry about the timing—just had to get it out. It is such a weight off my shoulders, and I am glad for Anne and you to know. I'm still the same old Carrie, but now you can stop looking for a husband for me. I would like to sit down and talk with Anne about it at more judicious moment in the future. I believe I'm going to feel a little awkward when I see her. Hope she will understand. I'm actually better as this Carrie because I am being true to myself, to all my friends, and hopefully soon to my entire family. Thanks for listening to my big bag of rocks.

You asked me yesterday what you do for me. You are a good listener, a good friend, and lots of fun, and you can ride a bike really well. You appear to be very nonjudgmental, and I feel secure in letting you in on my life story and all the changes I have made and am going through now. . . .

Whew . . . that took a gulp of air. Do we ever find out who we "really are," since we are ever changing? I get so scared sometimes about the course I've taken, wondering if it was right. I believe it was the honest way to go. I never wanted to hurt people in the process, but there was no way not to. Anyway, I like your company and I hope I don't wear you out with all my talking.

Carrie

PS: I went on my interview for the PTA program; just waiting to hear if I'm accepted.

From: *Charlie*
To: *Carrie*
Subject: *Thanks for listening*

Carrie,

I don't think I have ever met a person as honest and caring as you. You have a wonderful sense of humor and are really fun to be with. My greatest joy in life is to help others, so you give me much joy when I see that I can help. I think we are stuck with each other for a long time.

And I forgot to mention that you are a much better Carrie. I am still in awe of your courage in being true to yourself and also being true to all the others in the relationship. You are simply amazing to me. You can feel free to share anything with me.

I love the talk. Sometimes I don't hear because of wind noise, and sometimes I don't listen, but you are good at catching that. It must be from raising those boys.

I have my fingers crossed for your acceptance into the physical therapy asst. program. Let me know as soon as you know.

Charlie

Sam and I went through three stages of separation before our relationship derailed into obliteration with no chance of return. The first gap started out in the bed with dead air between us, then it progressed to separate rooms, and finally to him moving to the basement. Through all of this, there were days full of exhausted silence. When we did speak, our conversations were consistently negative, with threats of divorce slung in the air.

The day Sam left, it had just begun to rain—just like the day when Ryann walked into my life. A light rain, but one that creates enough water to make a tune on the branches and leaves in the trees before landing in the grass and creating mud puddles that put off a damp scent that sticks with you. Each time I smelled the sweet rain approaching after that, I remembered where I was years before, in transition.

Sam stood looking out the front door with his hand on the knob; I was at the top of the stairs stuck in a hazy stare between him and the rain. It had just started to drizzle and it was quite gray outside, and in that moment my heart felt so dark.

"If I leave this time, I'm not coming back!" he said. He had said that many times before, but everything about his threat today was different: the sound of his voice, his eyes, his facial muscles—he looked dreadfully tired but also unwavering.

I cowered behind the door at the top of the stairs and thought for a moment about the words I wanted to say: *leave, and don't come back.* But instead I put the fault back on him, saying, "I can't make you stay."

He looked up at me with a still calmness and shook his head from side to side before walking out into the rain, closing the door behind him. I wondered how such a basic movement could be so paralyzing. I lost track of time watching the drizzle become drops outside the window next to me, waiting for the front door to open followed by a slam and Sam's angry voice close behind. That was our usual pattern—but, as I said, that day was different.

After many moments passed and I gave up on Sam coming back, I staggered away from the steps to my room. I felt the heaviest I had ever felt in my entire life. It was so difficult to put one foot in front of the other—but somehow I managed to make it to the bed and collapse. I thought I could disappear as easily as he did, but it didn't work; the future he'd thought I was planning with him was still there, and for some reason it was magnified because he was gone. Needles pierced my thoughts from all the lies I'd let grow in my heart, and I wondered if I would ever be able to laugh again. I lay there alone, sick to my stomach and sobbing, filled with feelings of his final departure.

———

I was still lingering in my squealing loneliness on the bed when I heard the front door close with a resounding *bam*. My stomach blew up with butterflies and I jumped to my feet. I wiped my eyes and tried to look strong, wondering if Sam was back. Then I heard more than one pair of feet, and I knew it was the boys. *How am I going to tell them their Dad's not coming home tonight?*

Quinn ran in the room first, with Nelson trailing close behind. The panic I was feeling told me there was no way I would be able to keep my despair intact; I would have to tell them. I got up and put my arms out, motioning for them to come over.

Nelson sensed something was awry because instead of coming to me, he took a step back. "What's wrong?" he asked, suspicion in his voice.

"Yeah, what's wrong, Mom?" Quinn echoed.

Secretly I was glad they hadn't taken me up on the hug I was offering, because a hug would only have caused tears to well up.

I've never been the type to sit and talk when emotions are churning up a whirlwind inside me; I do much better if I move as I work through them out loud. I stood and walked toward the bedroom door. "We'll talk, but can we do it outside. The leaves are getting out of hand, and I could use some help raking."

"Yuck, I hate raking," Quinn said.

"Me too, and I have lots of homework," Nelson said.

"Please . . . I have something to talk to y'all about, and I could really use the help before it gets dark."

With just a little more persuading, they followed me down the stairs. I passed by the door Sam had opened and shut for the last time, and a cloudburst of goose bumps ran the length of my body. For some reason I had thought I would be comfortable in his absence, that I could somehow just close that chapter in my life without ever looking back. Silly me, thinking I could close that door—that would essentially be turning my back on my two children. I felt so emotionally tarnished in that moment; I had no idea how I was going to be a capable adult and pull off talking to my boys about our new existence as a broken family.

It was cold outside and the wind was blowing the leaves in the yard all around us—not really the best day to rake. "Nelson, you look for the tarp," I said, opening the shed, "and Quinn, you get the rakes; I'll get the wheelbarrow."

"I always have to get the tarp," Nelson whined back.

"It's better than the rakes," Quinn said.

"Come on, guys—let's just get started raking," I said flatly.

I think the only reason they didn't put up a bigger fight about helping was because they knew there was something desperately wrong. They noticed that the air between their parents was quite stale, and that over the last year we had started sleeping in separate rooms. They were just standing by, waiting for me to drop the bomb. As we rummaged for our assigned items, we all fell mute, and in that silence I started playing games in my head, thinking, *Please let me revert to the days when I was just a carefree kid, about to have a good ol' time playing in the leaves.*

The boys stepped out of the shed with slumped shoulders and not as much bounce in their steps as usual. I was still in the shed looking down at them, and I was so impatient to "fix" things, I blurted out, "Your dad and I can't live together anymore."

Even before the last words came out, I thought to myself, *That wasn't very tactful.* Quinn dropped the rakes on the ground right where he was standing, and Nelson's shoulders slumped forward even further, so he was dragging the tarp on the ground, and he looked up at me with hurt in his eyes. His expression sent my mind back in time to when he was two, holding his "blankie." Back then, all he wanted was to be held, rocked, and told everything was going to be all right. I wasn't sure which one of us wanted to be held and rocked more in this moment, but I knew I sure could have used it. We were all wavering in and out of two states of being, adult and child.

A pile of leaves flew up and blew around us, and I wished I could wail out my hurt with the whirling leaves for the world to hear, but Quinn beat me to it.

"Mom, why are you so selfish?" he shouted, stomping his feet. "You're so mean. I don't want to live here without Dad."

"Me either," Nelson said, looking at me with tearful eyes.

I faced my palms outward where they dangled by my sides and opened all my fingers in a desperate, pleading way. "It doesn't mean we love you any less. It will actually be better; you'll get to spend time with both of us, and there won't be any yelling or fighting going on between us."

"I don't care about the yelling and screaming!" Nelson said. He threw the tarp down and ran back into the house, slamming the door with a big loud thud behind him—a sound that, given Sam's departure just a few hours earlier, made my stomach cramp up extra tight. Quinn turned and ran as well, leaving me alone with the leaves and one last heavy-duty punch trailing in the air behind him: "I don't like you!"

I felt swimmy-headed with anger and sadness, but I couldn't find the tears I needed to cry; I must have used them up earlier in the day. I also didn't have the energy to chase after my boys, so I stepped out of the shed and commenced to raking. With the first scrape of the rake against the dry ground, I thought, *Boy, this is going to be a long evening,* and with that, a fountain of salty tears came loose from their hiding place. Leaves and tears were all I saw until it got too dark to see anything at all. I wished for a full autumn moon so I could hide outside all night, raking, but the moon was far from full.

With no excuse to be outside anymore, I dragged my aching heart back into the house to face the boys once more. It wasn't happening as I'd hoped it would; I wanted us all together in one room so I could help the boys understand why their parents couldn't live in the same house anymore.

"Please come out so we can work through this," I pleaded through their closed bedroom doors. "Or can you at least come out for dinner?"

"No, I don't want to talk," Nelson snorted forcefully through his tears.

I leaned my head on Quinn's door, waiting for an answer, but only heard silence. I searched around in my mind for the best words to say, and all I could come up with was a poor, pitiful, "Please . . ."

This time Nelson answered louder and without any sign of sobs, "No, I'm not coming out!"

I realized I could only listen to empty air for so long. For now, it was best to leave them and let them be with their thoughts. "Well, when you are ready to talk, let me know. I'm going to make spaghetti; it will be on the kitchen table when you feel like coming down and eating."

I walked down the stairs. Quinn's door opened as I reached the landing. "I'm not coming down to eat or talk," he shouted nervously as he went from his room to Nelson's.

Having no idea when or if the boys would come downstairs, I went into the kitchen to prepare our meal and respect their whispering silence. When the food was ready, I put two bowls of spaghetti on the table and retreated to my room.

On my bedside table was the mail I had brought in earlier in the day. Glowing on the top of the pile was a letter from South College. I hadn't had a chance to open it before the boys came barreling into the house and our world spun into an emotional tailspin. Now I sat down on the bed, picked up the letter, and slowly flipped it back and forth, considering the changes it could be holding inside. Then I slipped into my sarcastic, Debbie Downer role: *All I need now is to finish this day with a rejection letter from South College.*

I took a deep breath, blew out my cheeks, and told myself to hush and open up the letter. If it had been any other day, I would have ripped the envelope open fast without so much as a thought, but today I was robotically slow about tearing the top open and removing the letter. Holding the paper in hand, I scanned each line quickly to find the only word I cared much about reading: *accepted.* There it was.

I set the letter down gently on the table and turned out the light. Before falling asleep I thought to myself, *Sometimes in life you don't know what you can do until you have to go through it.*

13
Forgiveness

You know I think I'm a stronger person for realizing you can't make everybody love you.

—Clay Aiken, born November 30, 1978, Raleigh, North Carolina

I started the physical therapy assistant program soon after Sam left, and Charlie made it through that spring and summer riding a bike really well despite his increasing heart issues. He had meant it when he'd said he was a survivor. His zest for life was alive and well; he did everything with fervor and intensity, just as I hoped to do each day with my life from then on. Charlie was having truly legitimate issues with his heart, while I was having truly legitimate issues with heartbreak. I woke every day thankful that he had entered my life and prayed we had many more days on the black pavement together.

It's amazing what biking can do for the soul and body, especially when you have friends to share it with. It becomes therapy: your endorphins begin to bounce around, sending all your troubles into the wind, where they float into the ears of your buddies on their bicycles. It's an intriguing journey: you never know, from one ride to the next, what surprises may be waiting around the switchbacks. Think about it: one curve I was straight, and the next I was gay (as far as Charlie was concerned, anyway). It's hard to know what the person next to you is holding deep inside.

From: Carrie
To: Charlie
Subject: Worried

Charlie,

You know I have to worry especially when you turn down a ride because your heart is tapping a new tune. Thanks for calling and putting my mind to rest. I was going to call but you beat me to it. I am so happy to hear things are back to the old beat. Please monitor and take care . . . I'm looking forward to many more years of riding and babbling all my worries to you.

What did you and the doctors at Duke decide on the pacemaker?
Carrie

From: Charlie
To: Carrie
Subject: Worried

Carrie,

Duke was wonderful, and I have decided to return in two weeks to get the pacemaker and spend some more time there on other issues with my heart. The head of arrhythmia ablation services spent over half an hour with Anne and me to decide on a plan. Anne has convinced me that I should listen to the doctors here and at Duke and stay off my bike on the road until I've gotten the pacemaker. They say you never know when a five-second pause will turn into a ten with passing out. I am setting up my trainer and will go to spin class.

Don't worry. I am a survivor. Your babbling is fascinating to me, so keep it up.
Charlie

Charlie went to Duke and got his pacemaker. He was back on the road a couple of weeks later, and we made it through the short tunnel of awkwardness that I felt after revealing my secret to him.

It was a beautiful fall day for biking. The morning was a bit chilly, but nothing a windbreaker couldn't take care of. There were fifteen people on the ride with us—a thirty-four-mile route that left out of Weaverville, north of Asheville.

I was in desperate need of a bike ride that morning, and I felt it deep inside. The car ride up to Weaverville was about twenty-five minutes, which gave me plenty of time to replay the day before over and over in my mind: Sam was contesting our divorce, so we'd spent the day in the Buncombe County courthouse, waiting on the judge to assign us a date and case number. If we didn't reach an agreement by that assigned date, we would be back in the courtroom with the judge, making the decision on how to split our assets. But if the feelings living deep within me had a way to speak, I think they would have cried out for much more than the simple task of separating money.

I arrived a few minutes early at the courthouse and sat down on an old wooden bench that resembled a worn-out church pew. After a few minutes of being alone with my anxiety, I watched a single-file line of prisoners in orange jumpsuits with chains around their ankles shuffle by. The clank and drag across the wooden floors sent my mind into a spiral of self-pity and resentment about my predicament.

Once I was in the courtroom, my body flooded with shakes and I experienced the entire hearing as one big, foggy delusion. I woke only when my lawyer nudged my shoulder and motioned for me to stand. The judge barked out a date and time, then, with what felt like a hatchet to me, the judge sliced our sixteen years together into an ending moment. I never looked at Sam, not even when I left the room; I didn't have the courage to.

I was in tears by the time I pulled into a spot in the Weaverville Municipal lot. I pulled in a little too far, and my tires bounced off the parking block, shaking me out of my thoughts about my day in the courtroom. Jack, a retiree who organized the weekly club rides, liked leaving promptly at the listed start time, so I put my car in park, wiped away my tears the best I could, and stumbled out onto the pavement.

"I'll make it . . . I'm not late," I called out.

The other fifteen riders, all of whom were ready to go, shot me a familiar look that didn't need any words: *Sure, you're going to make it,* the look said. They were used to me arriving just in time, and then making a quick race to the bathroom. Today was no exception.

When I came back from the bathroom, the riders were all introducing themselves, as ritual had it whenever there was someone new in the bunch. I entered the circle beside a new rider about to introduce herself. She had soft, warm eyes and long, curly brown hair, looked to be in her late fifties, and was really skinny, like a pole bean. Her body language was melancholic, and her pleasant expression obviously masked something worrisome. "I'm Jackie," she said quietly. "I've just moved to the area from Pennsylvania."

After I introduced myself—I was the last to go—Jack quickly went over the safety rules for the ride and pointed out where the first stop would be for regrouping. On club rides we tried to go by the policy of no rider left behind, unless the riders had cue sheets and preferred to ride at their own pace.

Together, we meandered in a single-file line out of the parking lot and north up Main Street. The streets were full of colorful leaves that crackled under our tires. I made a point of squeezing in behind Jackie with every intention to inquire about her story; I didn't want to be stuck in my head listening to my own story for the next few hours. But I decided I would wait for about three miles, until we were off the main roads, to begin my onslaught of questions.

We turned left onto Salem Hill Road, and at the first sign of incline, we spread out to climb at our own pace. I quickly pedaled out of the line and pulled up beside Jackie.

Gulping for air, I choked out the classic Southern greeting: "Hey."

"Hi," she replied.

"How do you like Asheville?" I asked her.

Her skinny structure suggested she was a good climber—and she was. I was already trying to keep my heavy breathing undercover. Without being too obvious about it, I was also trying to wipe away the black mascara streaks peeking out from under my riding glasses, exposing the evidence of my tears.

"It's beautiful," Jackie said, "but I'd like to be here under different circumstances."

"Well, what might those circumstances be that brought you here?"

She was a little hesitant in her reply—rightfully so, we had met each other less than thirty minutes earlier. But knowing the timing must have been perfect for her to contribute a big detail like "under different circumstances," I knew I had to be a busybody right away to get the particulars out of her.

Jumping in to try and make her feel comfortable with me, I blurted out, "I'm going through an awful divorce and just can't seem to hold myself together. The only things that are keeping me halfway in order are my boys and school. They're depending on me, and I'm depending on my degree."

"That's why I'm here," she replied quickly. "My husband left me a letter back in Pennsylvania on the kitchen counter telling me the many ways he was unhappy, so I left that day with the letter and my bags. I didn't beg him to stay or ask if we could try to make it work; I just walked away, and this is my second divorce."

"How long has it been since you left?" I asked.

"Just a little over three weeks."

"Why Asheville?"

"My daughter and her husband and two girls live here."

Given that Jackie was older and probably wiser, this seemed like a perfect opportunity to seek advice from someone who might have answers to my many questions. "Please tell me it gets better," I begged. "We've been separated for over seven months and I'm still wallowing in my defeat. *Is* this defeat, or is that just my perception because I'm so new at this?"

Jackie didn't answer my question right away. She rode silently next to me as we slowly approached the rise of the hill, and remained silent as we began our descent. I could feel the wind pull the falling leaves to the back of my bike, making a visible whirlwind of color behind me. At the bottom, I stopped and waited for Jackie. She came down the hill, beautifully composed, and gingerly stopped right beside me. She was riding a turquoise Cannondale that seemed to be an older steel bike. Her shoes were sandals, and I noticed her toenails were painted the same turquoise as the bike. This told me one thing for sure: she was a bike junkie, just like the rest of us.

"Aren't your feet cold?" I asked.

"No, my feet are fine," she said with deep conviction. "Remember, I'm from up north; it's a lot colder there this time of year." She paused and studied me for a second, and then finally addressed the question I had asked her a few minutes earlier. "This is my second divorce and I wish I could tell you it gets better, but I don't know that it does. The pain changes and you learn to live in the midst of it. You must find the courage and power in your heart to forgive everyone involved and move on."

Frustrated, I started squeezing my handlebars hard in a circular motion, round and round, feeling the handlebar gel shifting under my hands. "What happens if you forgive them but you can't find the courage to forgive yourself?"

There was a bit of a pause between us as the wind picked up some leaves and splashed them right in front of us. I had a look of puzzlement on my face, but Jackie didn't. She pursed her lips into a fragile grin, shrugged her shoulders, and said, "I think I said *everyone* involved."

14
Traveling North

The mountains were his masters. They rimmed in life.
They were the cup of reality beyond growth, beyond
struggle and death. They were his absolute unity in the
midst of eternal change.

— *Look Homeward, Angel,* by Thomas Wolfe, born October 3, 1900,
Asheville, North Carolina

About four months after I met Jackie, I was still struggling to come to grips with my separation and decided to get out of town for a few days. I made the three-hour trip north to West Virginia to visit Susan and Jim, very dear friends from Sam's medical school days. I met Jim, who was a counselor, and Susan, who was a speech therapist, at my first job out of college, as a recreational therapist at the local developmentally disabled facility. The four of us had become instant friends.

I lied to my sons about this trip and told them I was going to visit my dad in South Carolina, because I didn't want them to speculate that I was going to visit Ryann in West Virginia. I was paranoid that the boys knew about my affair with her, and I was so stuck in that lunacy that I was always on edge. It didn't matter if I had covered up all the deceit—physically and mentally—I went over the thought of being found out over and over again, my mind turning faster than the cogs on my bicycle.

Just the thought of traveling north without Ryann being at the end of the trip was hard for me. Almost every time I drove north of Asheville (usually to ride my bike in Yancey and Madison Counties), it brought back flashbacks of my lost love. These hallucinations could send me into a deep depression that took days to climb out of.

After a year of too many good-bye threats, Ryann and I had made a final decision to not speak with one another anymore. For that first year, because we refused to give up on one another so quickly, we both became very familiar with the Virginia towns halfway between West Virginia and North Carolina. Even if we could only manage to slip away for a few hours, we did it, hoping to smother our withdrawal from one another just a bit. But it never seemed to be enough. We were always constructing elaborate plans to get to one another and steal weekends together before having to face our families once more with guilt in our hearts and on our faces.

This trip would be a bittersweet juncture and a test of my emotional strength. Could I hold it together?

From: Charlie
To: Carrie
Subject: *West Virginia*

Carrie,

I hope I did not make you crazy and lose sleep last night. It was an accident when I mentioned West Virginia. I really meant to say South Carolina. I did not dwell on it and it may be something to speak with Quinn about, he did look a little surprised and upset when I mentioned it.

One thing I do want to work with him on is having him spend a little time on figuring out why people react to him the way they do. He tends to get upset about small things, like the clothing rules at school, and does not understand his grades. He needs a better understanding that people are not like computer games and react in different ways every time depending on a whole bunch of things going on in their lives. If he can figure out what motivates other people and forget getting so upset, he will be very successful.

Is this an okay subject? You are his mom and can decide where my emphasis should be.

I want to help, not make things worse.
Charlie

From: *Carrie*
To: *Charlie*
Subject: *Worried*

Charlie,

How can you make somebody crazy if they already are crazy? I wish I had all the answers, but no . . . not I! I'm having such a hard time handling my situation, West Virginia, and the boys. I have a feeling Sam has told them the very thing they don't want to believe, that their mom is having an affair with a woman and it happens to be Ryann back in West Virginia. My heart aches when I don't tell the truth, and this truth could open a big can of worms. I don't know if I am or the boys are ready for this . . . I just don't know Charlie???? It makes me shake all over thinking about it.

I think the subject you are going to approach with Quinn is a good one. Quinn needs tolerance for constructive criticism. He has to understand not everyone approaches in a positive manner. He gets frustrated very easily with discipline and manners. Be aware he may give you a little resistance—always does with me when I broach this subject.

Sorry I was short on the phone earlier. I was trying to muster up some energy for a bike ride in the woods.
Carrie

I was still having a hard time kicking Ryann out of my mind; it was if a true tug-of-war game was going on up there. I knew the best thing for me to do was to completely close the door on her, but my heart wouldn't let go. I was quite naive when it came to her. I thought I could will her to leave her husband, and that if she just did that, we could move in together and live with our children happily ever after. After all, I had left Sam; why couldn't she leave Jim?

It took a long time, but I finally realized Ryann was not ready to make that change and she would just come to resent me if I kept pushing her in that direction. A decision of that magnitude had to be made by Ryann alone, and no matter how much love I gave her, I couldn't make it happen any faster. I had to trust that the strength of her love for me would help her leave at her own pace and travel to her own destination. Only time would tell if I was on the other end at the right moment.

It had been a year since I'd traveled up Sam's Gap on my way to Virginia. Every time before this, I'd been full of such sweet, quivering anticipation as I drove this road, excited to get into Ryann's arms. There were times when I was stalled by a wreck and my mind would play tricks on me: the cars on the opposite side of the highway would appear to be moving in extreme fast-forward motion. Heart-stricken with panic, I would open my road atlas and locate side roads I could take instead, desperate to prevent what precious little time I had from slipping away. After all, we had only a few hours in Damascus to ride our mountain bikes on the Creeper Trail, or to explore the roads of Washington County. If it was too cold to ride, we would have lunch with one another before jumping back on the highway and heading in opposite directions, toward home.

Ryann always brought books along in case it rained. We found a remote parking lot down a side road by some woods and a small creek, and she would read to me over the light patter of rain on the roof of the car as we lay holding each other tight in our arms. I'd watch the drops grow bigger as they ran down the windows before rolling out of sight while her gentle voice told a story from someplace far away, in another time. Tangled up in each other's arms, our hearts and our minds were taken somewhere else, and it fooled us into thinking we were together. But we always had to go back; that was *our* story.

"Promise to always read to me," I would say, my voice laced with hope.

"I promise," she would answer back with conviction and a soft kiss.

We met in Damascus so frequently that we were on a first-name basis with the local bike shop owner and most restaurants in town. The owner of the burrito shop would sit and have an occasional beer with us and discuss small-town politics. They accepted us without knowing our details. The only information they had about us was that I had ventured northeast from Asheville and she had traveled southwest from Bluefield. They had no idea when the two lesbians without a background were going to roll into town. Being in a town with no history had its advantages: we were each other's secrets back home, but in Damascus we could belong to one another for a few short hours.

I'd make every attempt not to cry as we hugged before breaking our embrace to get in our cars, knowing my tears would only upset Ryann—but I was not a master of hiding my emotions, especially when it came to good-byes.

I'd often get angry and reach for both her hands, hold tight, and plead, "You're going back to an intact family; this has to be easier for you. My family is all broken up and I don't have the security that you have anymore."

"You always destroy the time we've had together," she'd say, pulling away. "Just learn to be happy in the moment."

"Are we ever going to be together?"

"Yes, I promise in time I will leave."

The instant I got on the road and out of Ryann's sight, I would swing between crying and grinning the majority of the way home. The crying stemmed from missing her and wanting more; the grins from thoughts of the playful moments we had just experienced together. It would all come to a head when I reached the switchbacks that brought me back down Buckner Gap into North Carolina. Like clockwork, I'd usually start wailing like a baby. When my wails became so intense that I started to scare myself, I played the radio really loud, hoping it would just slightly drown out my unrelenting sobs. I figured it was all right to be crazy alone because no one could hear me, and it was best to get it out before I got to the boys. More often than not I would be late to pick Quinn and Nelson up from school on these days. I have no idea how I didn't get any tickets on 81 or 26 as I sped through three states to get back home.

Ryann usually called at least once if not five times on the trip back. My heart went through ripples in sync with her rings, and I'd grab a tissue to blow away my sobs before answering.

"Hello," I'd say, disguising my voice with happiness.

After a moment of silence she'd answer back, "Hey, I just thought I would check on you. Are you doing okay?"

"I guess as good as I'm going to be when leaving you," I'd say. I wasn't a good liar; there was no point in pretending. "I already miss you. I don't know, Ryann, sometimes I think it would be better not to see one another and wait until we can get a long weekend. It's like we're teasing each other with just a small taste."

"I know, I can still taste you on my lips."

"Me too, I can still feel your arms and body touching me."

We would go back and forth like this, tormenting one another, trying to reinforce our love for one another on the phone. A love I somehow thought could become more than an affair. I never told Ryann how much I really hurt on the way home, knowing it would only push her away. That was the last thing I wanted to do.

Calm would finally take over when I saw the Buncombe County signs. At that point I would lock Washington County up in a separate compartment in my mind, and I'd keep it there until the next time we were able to sneak away to meet halfway between our homes.

Now, as I sped north on Route 81 to visit Susan and Jim, a whole new feeling and meaning came over me. Just as I passed the Damascus exit, "Train Song," sung by Feist and Ben Gibbard, began playing on the radio. The lyrics brought Ryann right back to me, but this time, it wasn't painful; instead, a peaceful smile spread across my face. I coughed out giggles when they said something about traveling north; it made me think back to that spring day in Ira's Coffeehouse when two girls turned to the right instead of the left and a simple question became a life forever changed. The true-to-life lyrics echoed deeper in my ears along with the questioning cry of the guitar. I started hitting the steering wheel with the palm of my hand and tears began to pour down my face once again. I wondered where this vast well of tears was coming from, and whether they would ever stop. When I was with Ryann, it was like being in the wilderness: I wanted to run there forever, but reality called my name, and I had to somehow find the courage to make my way back from the fog I'd created.

I stared out the window at the same landscapes I had passed on all my deceptive trips north. "I'm still not over this!" I whispered out loud. "God . . . how long is this going to take me? Why can't you just stop loving someone and have it all get better? Why is the beginning and end so hard; is it because the middle is so good?"

I just wanted to get to Susan and Jim and feel safe in their home. I felt like a vulnerable, broken child inside, and I knew once I got to their home I would find peace and arms to hold me tight.

I skipped the rest of the song and found a tune that was upbeat and not chock-full of melodramatic lyrics. That helped me escape my pensive mood. After passing through the second tunnel on Route 77, I looked at the big highway sign overhead, which read WELCOME TO WILD WONDERFUL WEST VIRGINIA, and a deluge of affection for this beautiful place came over me. A fragile smile emerged on my face. After years of moving up and down the East Coast while Sam did internships and residencies, I had come to realize the people of West Virginia were the most welcoming of them all. This was where I created my first home completely independent of my childhood home— no more sidestepping with Mom and Dad. In 1988, I graduated with my bachelor's degree on December 17, married Sam on December 23, and moved to West Virginia the day after that. I didn't have any time to think; it was as if a whirlwind swept me off my feet and blew me from the mountains of North Carolina straight up to the mountains of West Virginia. I grew up there, in the creases of those mountains; it was where I built a family, and where I learned who I was and who I was not.

The next sign I saw on the highway read PIPESTEM STATE PARK; that turned my thoughts back to the many adventurous hikes I had with the boys there, and kept my mind occupied for another hour or so. The boys must have been seven and five when I took them on the first of our many hikes in there. Our favorite hike took us to the bottom of Bluestone Gorge and back up the other side to the patrol cabin on Bearwallow Ridge. It was close to ten miles in all, with a river crossing by foot at the midway point. It seemed like a lot to ask of two little boys, but I wanted them to learn to face challenges with gusto—and what better way to do that than to make yourself do something you never thought you could do?

—

An hour later, Susan and Jim's house—my favorite home away from home in West Virginia—came into view in the distance, a soft haze reflecting off their white stucco walls, and I felt a calm peace liberate my heart. When I pulled into the driveway and got out of the car, their cats ran with unruffled grace to the porch door, trying to disguise their curiosity even as they checked out the new visitor.

Before I could take two steps, my favorite dog, Saul, a hodgepodge mixed breed—what we called a Heinz Fifty-Seven back home—came to greet me wagging his whole body. He'd showed up one winter day on their front doorstep and worked his way into their hearts.

Saul licked me all over, finding every bit of exposed skin, and I worked hard not to fall down in the gravel. I looked up at the porch door to see Susan standing on her steps waving and hollering, "Hey girl, you made it."

My heart knotted up slightly, but in a good way. I stood up and looked to my friend from across the drive; my emotions were caught between laughter and blissful tears. I jumped up and took off in a fast trot to get to her. We reached each other about halfway down the path and latched on to one another tight. I think we were trying to see who could hug the hardest.

I turned sideways and intertwined my arm with hers, and then we started weaving up the path while playing bumper cars with our hips. "Yep, I finally made it—and I'm so happy to see you. Where's Jim?"

"He went to the store to get a few things for dinner."

"How was your trip?" she asked, pulling my arm back toward her side.

"Well beyond crying halfway here, it was pretty uneventful."

"Was it over him or her?"

I leaned my head on her shoulder. "I don't know, maybe both of them. I can't get any lucidity in my mind with the grief of losing her and the agonizing pain of leaving him."

She pulled me even closer. "Let's get inside and talk about it over some tea for a bit before Jim gets back."

Once inside, a wave of comfort bigger than the one I'd felt standing outside on the gravel driveway surrounded me. The walls were warm from the sunlight peering through the windows, and I inhaled the familiar smell of books, which were strewn over any spare surface, including the piano, which was almost bigger than the room itself. Native West Virginian arts were thrown in the mix, and the familiar brown chaise lounge was in the same spot I remembered, with welcoming blankets awaiting my shoulders. This was one of the most unique places I had ever been to, and I absolutely loved it.

Susan made it across the room to the small kitchen and started rummaging in the cabinets for tea and cups. I could barely hear her over all the shuffling around in the cabinets, but I just made out her muffled words: "I have green tea with mint, Berry Zinger, and Lemon Zinger. Which do you fancy?"

"The Berry Zinger sounds fine."

I stepped over to the chaise and plopped my emotionally exhausted body down. "Has Jim heard from the medical school yet?" He had been contemplating going to medical school for a few years, but it had taken a bit of encouragement and persuasion to get him to make the final jump and actually apply.

"No," Susan said, "and this waiting game is awful. You have to put so much of your life on hold."

The teakettle started singing its whistle, and I tried to speak over it. "I know—I remember when Sam was waiting to hear."

"Well, how is the physical therapy assistant program coming along?" she asked loudly from the kitchen.

"It's pretty intense right now because I'm in the home stretch. I detest Kinesiology the most, but I'm sure I will somehow get through it. Just a couple more months of it. I can't believe how fast it's gone by. Between going to school, trying to raise my boys, and my separation from Sam, I feel like I'm in a fog half the time."

She patted the top of the kitchen table. "Come on over and let's have some tea while you get your worries out of your head and on this table right now."

"I'll be right over if you promise to play the piano afterward." I had such fond memories of her playing while the boys ran through the house acting like monkeys in a jungle. Even with all their ruckus, she never batted an eye or missed a note. I just sat back on the lounge enjoying the competing ambience of the boys going wild with their toys and the classical music bouncing from wall to wall.

"It would be an honor to play a tune or two if it helps you heal a bit."

I nodded and pulled up a chair on the closest end of the table. Susan poured the hot water before sitting on the opposite side and saying, "Carrie, you're going to have to come to realize that some people have one great love of their life and others have more than one. You've managed to have two already."

"Well, I only wanted one," I said forcefully, "and I never knew I could be capable of loving someone as much or more than my first love. Sam was there through thick and thin. He was wonderful in so many ways, and he had reasons to walk, but he didn't."

"Where is your logic going here, Carrie? Why did he have reasons to walk?"

"For lack of better words, I think if only he had been a woman, we would have gotten along just fine and we wouldn't be apart. I still remember when he asked me to marry him a second time in that little church in Michigan."

"He did? Really?"

"Yeah, he was doing his OB/GYN rotation up there. For someone who had so little time, he managed to put on a full-blown fireworks show: he had friends bring me to the church, and he was inside waiting with the surprise question 'Will you marry me again?'"

Susan's eyes were wide. "Did it catch you off guard? What did you say?"

"Well, goodness me . . . what do you think I said?" I said sarcastically. "'No, I don't want to marry you again, because I'd rather be with a woman'? It crossed my mind, but only for a second. I said yes, of course."

"That's the best of romance—getting married twice," Susan said, a big smile on her face.

"It wasn't the most romantic scene. Nelson was crawling on the magenta carpet between the church pews, and we renewed our vows in shorts and T-shirts. It was three years after we first exchanged vows—to love each other in sickness and health, till death do us part. Both times I sealed those cowardly words with a kiss. You can't get more selfish than that. It just sent me deeper into the closet and him deeper in love with someone he thought he knew."

"Do I detect a little anger mixed up in all that love?"

"You sure do, and lots of it. I don't want to fail to mention that he was a very attentive dad even though he had so little time. Sometimes I don't know how he did it, working such long hours with as little as an hour or two of sleep. And then he'd come home and be there for all of us—and I mean *be there*."

"Good," Susan said. "Anger means you're on the second stage of grief and you only have three more to go. Not that I ever thought Ryann was worth your grieving too much over, but you have two children with Sam, and that may take a little extra grieving."

I wasn't surprised by Susan's comment; she had become my confidant after my affair with Ryann ended, and I knew I hadn't painted a perfect picture of Ryann. The image I had presented to Susan wavered between Edvard Munch's *The Scream* and Van Gogh's *Starry Night*, depending on how broken my heart was at any given moment. The *Scream* images had to be the ones that had jaded her view of Ryann the most.

"Susan, it's not funny—I think there are days when I'm losing my mind and I'm barely able to breathe. I feel like I'm drowning in the quicksand of Ryann and Sam and trying to figure out what it all means and why I did what I did."

"I know it's not funny and I know it's not easy, but what you don't seem to understand is that we all have days that are hard for whatever reason—it's part of life. These are the basics: you can't have the good without the bad, and it won't get any better if you fight the withdrawals of lost or diminished love."

"You're right . . . but it's the silent moments that grab me, when I'm alone and no one is around. In those moments, Sam and Ryann drift in to my mind like the tide coming in. But I will say, the more distance I put between us, the easier it seems to get. I know it will just take time; after all, that is all we have, right? *Time.*"

Susan sipped her tea and looked across the table at me with an intent look   a look she saved for special occasions. It said, *Listen to me*, without actually using the words.

I let out a slight *grrr* and said, "I'm really trying, Susan, and there are days when I think I'm over it and that I've moved on . . . and then my heart begins to stagger and stumble like it did today in the car on the way up here." I covered both eyes with the palms of my hands and inhaled deeply before sighing out, "The forgetting is what is so difficult."

Susan reached over to my forearm and lightly rubbed it with her fingers. "You're asking too much by trying to figure out what it all means at this point in time. Let your emotions come as they do, embrace them, be with them, and then let them go—it will all untwine in time."

—

Susan played the piano that afternoon while I took a long, deep nap and dreamed good dreams. Jim was home by the time I woke up, and we all enjoyed dinner together that evening before sitting and sipping wine on the patio at dusk. It was so very remote and serene at their home. We listened to the coyotes in the distance and stayed outside until the sun went down and the moon came up. As I stared up at the multitude of stars above us, I felt in my heart that with or without Sam or Ryann, I was going to make it, because I had good friends to help me along the way.

15
Up in Flames

I'm like an old dog, I hate to be run off from home.

—Doc Watson, born March 3, 1923, Deep Gap, North Carolina

On my way home from my visit to West Virginia, I was acutely aware that it was the first time neither Sam nor Ryann would be there when I arrived. It was a trip for only me—to my own destination. As I had driven north to West Virginia, my vulnerability had felt very much alive in my bloodstream, but now that I was on my way home, that feeling dissipated and fluttered away like a butterfly. I was thankful that I had found the strength to know my marriage was truly over, and that I was on the cusp of a new life. It had turned out to be a much-needed, healing trip.

There was just one week left of the court-mandated year of separation from Sam. The part that continued to take a toll on my heart was that in living separate lives, we were going to be halving the emotions that had evolved between us as spouses and parents.

When I got home, I sat down at my desk to send an e-mail to Charlie about my trip to West Virginia, hoping it would help me forget about the divorce mediation I knew I had to attend the next day.

From: Carrie
To: Charlie
Subject: West Virginia Trip

Charlie,

I'm including some photos from my trip because I wanted you to see why they call West Virginia "Wild and Wonderful." The majority of these were taken on my friend's property. We sat on their patio Saturday night and could hear coyotes howling in the valley. You think you have bears—Susan counted sixteen over the summer.

I had a wonderful mini-vacation, including a twenty-five-mile and seventeen-mile road ride, dinner in Lewisburg at a really nice restaurant, Stardust Café, and my first full-body massage at a bed and breakfast in Marlinton, West Virginia. My friends pampered me the whole time I was there. They gave me the cradling time I needed to contemplate my divorce and to know there's a light at the end of this long, trudging tunnel. It was a wonderfully selfish and decadent weekend.

If you and Anne ever want a weekend away in a marvelous town full of history it would be a fun trip, and my friends have invited everyone. There is also a lot for Anne to do, including arts and culture. I have a friend who is willing to lead us on road rides in the area too. Just a bit of food for thought.

So how was cycling across the state? I bet you're sleeping your week of cycling through the beautiful Piedmont off, and I can't wait to hear all about it. I've missed you and hope you saved a little energy to ride this coming weekend; I'm going to need it after tomorrow. Hopefully Sam and I will get things settled through mediation tomorrow and not end up in court.
Carrie

From: *Charlie*
To: *Carrie*
Subject: *West Virginia Trip*

Carrie,

Cycle North Carolina was great, but I'm sure glad I slept in a hotel. I'm including a summary that I sent to a lot of people.

I just finished Cycle North Carolina. The ride was from Black Mountain (15 miles east of Asheville) to Wingate, NC over four days at about sixty miles per day. You had the option of continuing for three more days to reach the ocean at Oak Island. There were over 1,000 riders in the event.

It was a different experience completely riding a multi-day ride rather than my short single-day rides, and it gave me great appreciation for the riders who do the twenty-day stage races of the Tour de France in Europe.

I rode a touring bike that is about three pounds heavier than my road bike and then added three pounds of touring gear, including a rack and big bag on the back. And, of course, I had to keep up with some friends who were twenty-five years younger and riding their normal road bikes, so I was putting out a lot of energy.

The first day was in the mountains with some long, painful climbs, so I was glad to hit the hotel. Next day was foothills and the last two days were like southern Minnesota flats (some hills at rivers). The mornings were cool and foggy and really beautiful as the sun came up when we were leaving the start each day. I had to remember one glove to wipe the nose and the other to wipe the glasses. The last day, I rode extra slowly to savor the last ten miles of the trip.

I can't tell you how much I feel honored in sharing the details of your life with me. It is a trust that I honor. Life has a way of working itself out. Sometimes I feel like I should comment more, but then I remember you don't always want solutions; you just want someone to listen.

Put away your worries about tomorrow. It will come and go, and we will get on a bike once again. Call me when things settle down, and we will plan a ride.

Charlie

My aunt Rosemary came to town in May 2006 to attend my pin-
ning and graduation from my physical therapy assistant program,
which just happened to fall on the same weekend my divorce was
going to hopefully reach a settlement. It seemed like I was destined
to do things in double: I had graduated from college and gotten married within one week, and now I was doing it again, but with a twist—
instead of graduation and marriage, graduation and divorce.

Sam was on his third attorney; he kept firing one and hoping the
next would tell him something better or give him different news than
the one before. He wouldn't agree to anything our attorneys sent back
and forth to reconcile our case. Now our day of mediation had arrived,
and if we were unable to solve our differences, it would be left up to
a judge to make a decision the very next day about what was best for
us as a family.

I was so happy my aunt was in town—she was extra good at plac-
ing her big arms around me with exactly the right amount of squeeze.
She would be my security blanket.

The morning of our mediation day, I had a really awful headache
from tossing all night. My mind was racing with questions. Had I
made the right decision or the wrong one? Hoping to hide my sweaty,
trembling hands, I kept one hand under my thigh and put the other
on the steering wheel as I drove to the meeting. I didn't want my aunt
to think I was crazy because I had the shakes—although it did seem
to me that it would take only a slight nudge for me to lose it and fall
over the edge without the mindset to recover.

The pressure in my head intensified. "Do you mind if we stop at the
drugstore on the corner, so I can get something for my headache?" I
asked, glancing at my aunt.

"No, not at all, honey," she said quickly. "Anything to make you feel
like you can handle and make it through the day."

"This is just going to be really hard, Aunt Rosemary."

"I know it is, honey, but just keep in mind this will all be over
tomorrow."

"Have you forgotten how difficult Sam can be?" I snapped back, as

I pulled into a parking space. "He could not agree to anything, and we could end up in court tomorrow."

"But I have a good feeling about today," Aunt Rosemary said, rubbing my shoulders.

I unbuckled my seat belt and swung open my door. "I hope you're right," I said before staggering out of the car and heading for the store.

My focus vanished instantly when I stepped through the drugstore's automatic doors; I forgot what I'd gone in for, and started wandering up and down the aisles, feeling lost. My mind was turning in circles, and my stomach was becoming a tornado of nausea. Today was it—there would no longer be Sam and Carrie living happily ever after. But how was I forgetting that we had been so unhappy for such a long time before this? I was losing my perspective, full of nostalgia for all the amazing times we had spent together as a family. My heart felt like it was going to thrash its way out of my chest; with every step I could feel a thump against my rib cage.

I must have looked frazzled and desperate, because as I was making my way up the shampoo row, a clerk in a blue vest looked directly at me and said, "Can I help you? Are you lost?"

Embarrassed, I looked down at the ground. "No, I'm just looking, thank you," I said, and quickly disappeared down the aisle, back into the abyss of my emotions.

I made it back to reality for a moment and remembered why I was there; I started heading toward the row of anti-inflammatories. But as I was getting close, a fountain of tears began to make its way up my chest and into my throat, and I knew if I didn't do something quick to distract myself, the flood was going to bust the levee and pour from my eyes.

Just when I thought there was no chance of stopping myself from sobbing uncontrollably, a Chia Pet appeared on the shelf in front of me. Realizing this was my opportunity to coax my mind away from self-pity, I began singing "Ch-ch-ch-chia" over and over in my head, and continued to do so until I found the Advil and got out of the store.

I practically ran to the register and became angry with the

automatic doors for not opening fast enough as I made my way back outside. It was as if I had been deprived of oxygen the whole time I was in the store and it wasn't until the outside air hit my face that I could breathe again. I inhaled deeply and fled the rest of the way to the car.

"Ch-ch-ch-chia!" I blurted out as I opened the car door.

My aunt looked over at me with wide eyes. "Well . . . did you see a Chia Pet inside?"

"Yep, it just brought back some old memories," I said, collecting myself. I paused and stared at the steering wheel in silence for a few beats before starting the car. My mind was interrogating itself, and I couldn't find any answers.

"Aunt Rosemary, I'm really nervous about today," I said after we'd driven two blocks, breaking the silence. "I hope I can make it without having a breakdown in front of everyone."

She took my hand. "You've made it this far. I'm sure the road was rocky and there were days you thought you wouldn't make it, but look at what you have accomplished in such a short time. You're much stronger than you know. I promise I will only be a phone call away if you need me."

I knew she meant it and she would bust the doors down to come to rescue me if I needed it. "Thank you," I said, squeezing her hand. "I need this reassurance now. It just hurts so much, going through this whole process."

—

The mediator's office was on a really busy road in Asheville, right next door to a strip club. It seemed ironic—this really well-kept Cape Cod law office next door to a dark and dilapidated strip club. I wondered who had put up the tall, brown, slatted wooden fence separating the worlds of right and wrong: a lawyer or a stripper.

When we pulled up, Sam was getting out of his car. It had been three months since I had seen him up close. He looked sad and tired, but he showed determination as he pushed the car door closed with the force of his briefcase. I looked over at my aunt and pulled my bottom lip out and down to gesture a sadness I couldn't find words for. I was also afraid that if I said anything, I would finally release a fountain of tears. That was probably what I needed to do, but the timing was all wrong.

"Breathe," she said.

And that's exactly what I did: I let out a really heavy sigh and sat in the car for a few more minutes. When I felt ready, I said good-bye to my aunt and went into the office alone.

My feet were heavy with panic and fear; it took extra energy to carry them up the steps and through the door. My attorney was waiting on me inside, and as soon as I walked in, he reached for my elbow and with his other hand pointed to a room to the left of the receptionist desk.

"We will be in this room, Carrie," he said, and steered me toward the door.

I could see that Sam was already situated in a room to the right. The rooms were separated by glass walls and doors, with a large common room in the middle. His gray, hazy silhouette was slightly hidden behind white eyelet curtains, but not quite enough for my breaking heart. I wished the curtains were solid so I wouldn't have to feel his pain mix with mine and twirl my gut into a tight little vortex. I could see that he was huddled in deep conversation with his attorneys already—I supposed to get this agonizing task over with as quickly as possible.

I told my attorney a week earlier when we were speaking of time and place that Sam and I would never come to an agreement with one another if we were in the same room. I had a deep-seated fear that as soon as things got started, he would bolt, as he had done so many times in the past.

We entered our room, which had a long black table and eight upright chairs. I guessed that they kept things cold and stiff in hopes that it would hurry arguing couples on their way. It seemed like a rather large space for just my attorney and me. I knew it would be nice to get off my shaky legs.

John my attorney began explaining what was going to happen right away. "Sam's attorney, Lane Jacobs, and I agreed this was the best mediator in town to work on your divorce agreement, since you've been on quite a journey getting to this table. The mediator, David Wright, has an uncanny way of helping couples reach agreements so things don't end up in court. We also thought the separate rooms were just what we needed for you and Sam."

Just as I was about to reply, a towering, distinguished-looking man opened the door and entered the room. He walked straight over to me and reached out to shake my hand with a firm grip.

"Hello, David Wright, pleased to meet you; I'll be helping with your divorce agreement."

"Hey, Carrie Highley, nice to meet you also," I replied with what little voice I could find.

"Hi," David said to John in a rather friendly way before shaking his hand. An underlying companionship radiated between them.

We all stared at one another without words for what seemed like an eternity, though I knew it was only a few seconds; then we pulled out our chairs to sit down. The scraping cry of the wood legs on the tile floor echoed coldness.

"Before we get started on our work, I was told to send a very important message over from Sam," David said. He clasped both hands in front of him on the shiny table and carefully looked right into my eyes. "There is no easy way to say this . . . Sam said he loves you very much and he wants to reconcile."

I stared down at David's fingers, so neatly intertwined together in front of me; it was easier than focusing on his questioning eyes. My chest and throat were wound up so tight I thought I was going to suffocate from the pressure. I swallowed deep, hoping to catch a breath and stop my deafening heartbeat from pounding so loudly. The only other time in my life that I could remember having this much trouble getting my words out no matter how hard I tried was at my wedding rehearsal, when it was my turn to say, "I do." I had totally frozen up in a panic then, and now it was happening again.

John looked over at me as my mouth dropped open in shock. He knew there was no hope for an answer out of me, so he answered for me: "We are not here to talk about reconciliation; we're here to settle a divorce that is weighing heavily on a family."

David looked right into my eyes again. "Carrie, do you agree with this?"

John was right; I knew I couldn't go back no matter how badly I wished I could reconsider my marriage. But I still couldn't get any words out, so I just nodded my head in agreement.

"Okay then, let's get to work," David said, and he proceeded to explain what his role was going to be in our divorce agreement. It was business for him, and it seemed so quick and cutthroat. Sixteen years together, and now it was down to closing up shop in an hour or two. I don't know how I thought it could be any different. We needed to come to an agreement, and sooner rather than later, because I knew Sam was going to be upset when David went back to tell him I wasn't considering reconciling.

"I want you both to understand something about Sam: he needs to feel like he is in charge or he may walk out the door. Believe me—he is already on his third attorney," I said.

"We need to try to be very considerate with our approach to this one," John agreed, nodding his head toward David.

"We'll do all we can to not upset him," David assured us.

We went over our divorce decree, which covered all the pertinent things couples must separate and agree upon—child support, custody, alimony, and last but not least, property division. Sam had just finished his residency, so there wasn't much for us to divide; with all our moving, we had thinned things out on a regular basis. When Sam walked out, he'd said he didn't want the house or anything in it.

David sketched out what we wanted on a legal pad and left the room to go next door. He was gone for about fifteen minutes and then he was back. He went over what Sam wanted with us quickly; we marked through things and made different offers on new sheets of legal paper, and David disappeared out of the room again. It all seemed so surreal to me; I just wanted it to end so I could go home and start over.

After several rounds of this, David came back with an altered, weary look on his face. My throat and chest started to cramp up again.

"What's wrong?" I asked.

"You were right. Sam has a strange look in his eyes and he seems to be getting very angry. He quite firmly told me he wasn't dickering to purchase a car and he's not going to go back and forth like this all day. As I was leaving the room, I looked back at him, and he looked quite skittish, a little like a wild animal."

Just as he was going to explain more, the door of the other room opened and slammed, and I heard shuffling and loud talking in the common room. I was sure I could hear Sam's voice in the chatter. Then I saw gray shadows pass the curtains, heading for the front door. David got up and darted out of the room. John and I locked eyes with one another and frowned before pushing our chairs back at the same time, jumping up, and dashing to the blinds covering the windows overlooking the street. We each pulled one of the wooden slats down so we could see outside.

Sam was making a dash to his car, and his lawyer, Lane, was in hot pursuit.

I looked over at John at the exact same time he looked at me with his reading glasses propped on the end of his nose. He tilted his head downward so he could look just over the top of them and said, "Carrie, this is not good."

"I know," I responded. "I told you this was going to happen. What do we do now?"

"Watch," he said, shrugging.

We turned and peered back through the small space between the blinds. Both Sam's car doors were now open, and Sam and Lane were halfway in on either side, one leg dangling out on the ground. It looked like there was a small struggle going on in the car between them.

"I think Lane is trying to get the keys," John said.

"I think you may be right," I said, mesmerized by the struggle.

I glanced to my left and noticed a lady was standing on the front porch in front of David, who was also watching the exchange intently.

"Who is that lady?" I asked John.

"Oh, that's Jenny, a sheriff's deputy. Lane gets her help sometimes when he thinks he may have a difficult case."

"But she doesn't have a uniform on."

"Sure, that's because she is not on duty; she's here to offer support to Lane if he needs it."

"Does this mean there are other people who go to the divorce guillotine kicking and screaming all along the way?" I asked, feeling a bit better about my situation.

"Carrie, divorce is difficult no matter how amicable couples try to make it. Lane knew this one was going to be extra difficult, so he asked Jenny to be here today."

We looked back outside to see Lane backing his way out of the car and Sam immediately jumping out the other side. Sam looked utterly frustrated and exhausted. He leaned his body against the side of the car and cradled his head in his hands.

"Lane got the keys," John whispered.

"I know . . . I saw," I whispered back.

Then Sam threw his arms in the air and yelled something to his attorney before turning and beginning a fast trot down the gravel driveway toward the busy road. Jenny bounded down the steps to meet Lane at the bottom, and they exchanged a few words before she started running after Sam.

"Oh my . . . John, what are we going to do now?"

"No worries yet, Carrie. I have faith in Jenny. She is really good at getting people back to the table."

Jenny had on high platform shoes, and she was twisting her ankles in the potholes along the gravel driveway in her effort to catch up to Sam. They both turned right out of the driveway and faded into the traffic, and my heart started to sink once again. I felt this overwhelming responsibility for Sam's pain. I so wished he would understand I hadn't stopped loving him—it was just in a different way.

"Oh, I feel sorry for her," I said to John, sighing. "Sam can be hard to work with."

"Jenny is really good at her job, Carrie."

He gently put his hand on my shoulder and directed me out into the common room to meet Lane and David, who were just coming back in through the screen door. John's kind but firm touch gave me a moment of security that I needed. It reminded me of how my dad had intertwined arms with me when he led me down the wedding aisle sixteen years earlier.

"Lane, I'd like you to meet Carrie Highley," John said.

"Hi, it's nice to meet you," I said, shaking the hand he offered me. "I'm sorry it's on such a sour note."

I couldn't help but look beyond him, out the front door. I was hoping I would see Jenny and Sam coming back, but the only thing in sight was the traffic speeding by. I was really happy my aunt had decided to go shopping down the road while she waited for me, so she couldn't witness our foolish behavior.

The three attorneys' adrenaline was filling up the space in the room. They were speaking to me, but I was oblivious to the conversation, lost in a hopeful daydream, staring out the front door, until John called out my name over and over: "Carrie. Carrie. *Carrie.*"

I finally woke from my stupor, and when he saw he had my attention, he said, "Carrie, we were trying to pinpoint what set Sam off. Lane thinks Sam lost it right away when David told him we were here to settle the divorce and not here to reconcile—"

"I think he was trying to keep his emotions intact, but he was having a very difficult time of it, so he had to come up with an excuse to escape," Lane interjected. "My theory is, he used the issue about having him pay for college to get up and walk out. We were going over the issues you had sent back over, and suddenly he became completely irritated, pushed the papers back over to me, and said quite forcefully that college tuition shouldn't have to be written into the agreement, that you know he will pay for it. Then he calmly started stacking his papers up and slowly putting them in his briefcase. He blatantly ignored everything we were saying; it was as if he was on a mission. Once he got his things organized, he got up, pushed his chair under the table, and walked out of the room."

"This is what he has done for years. I'm used to it," I said.

"We're hoping Jenny will get him to agree to come back," David said, "because if we don't settle this today, you two are going to be in the courtroom tomorrow."

"Let's take the college tuition requirement out," I said, looking at John. Then I added, looking right at Lane, "I really don't fancy going to court, and I think all the other things in the agreement are pretty reasonable."

"Intelligently Sam knows this is good, but emotionally he's not able to handle it," Lane said.

Hearing that was like a punch to my heart. I knew I was hurting Sam, but to hear an objective party say it made it feel so real. More than ever, I sympathized with what Sam must be going through.

Lane went into the other room to get his computer and brought it into the common room. We all stood around gazing at the computer over Lane's shoulder while he changed the college tuition part in the agreement. Then the three attorneys started speaking lawyer jargon, and I got completely lost, so my eyes trailed out the window again, hoping I would see Sam coming back. All I wanted from Sam was enough to keep the boys in our home until they graduated from high school. It was the most stable environment they had been in since they were born, and I felt they deserved that much.

"Do what it takes to keep us there until 2012, when Quinn graduates from high school," I said in a monotone voice as I was staring out the window.

"But you're entitled to so much more, Carrie," John said. "You've been home for sixteen years and moving all over the place while Sam was able to establish a career; the court will see it that way."

Lane took in what John said and turned around in the chair to look at all three of us above him. It seemed odd to be discussing things of this nature with the supposed enemy staring at me. David frowned a little and shrugged.

"There are very few entitlements in life, and if I had any I gave them up with choices I made," I said, pointing out the window. "Just please make the changes."

Jenny and Sam were walking side by side up the driveway. They appeared to be silent, and Sam was fixedly staring at the ground. It was my turn to take the lead; I looked at John with tears in my eyes and reached for his forearm to escort him back to our room. I was sure if Sam saw me anywhere in the vicinity of his attorney, he would think the opposite of what was happening.

When we got back in our room, I couldn't hold it back anymore and let my tears flow. John promptly grabbed the tissues and offered me one.

"This must be hard for you to see all the time—people at their worst," I managed to say through my tears.

"It may have been when I was just starting out, but now, being older and wiser, I know it is a new beginning for so many people. It's all uphill from here, Carrie."

I chuckled through my tears. "You shouldn't say that to a cyclist, especially a hill slug. The hills are the worst part of the ride."

We sent the agreement back and forth a couple more times before we reached the final contract. About an hour later, I signed, Sam signed, and the three attorneys made it official. My aunt came and picked me up when it was over, and I took her to the airport that afternoon. She gave me enough of her big hugs to last me a long time as we bade each other good-bye.

—

That night, the boys were with Sam and I was at home alone. I chose to celebrate my new beginning with a campfire. Instead of mourning my loss, I was going to eulogize the naive girl that I had been. It was time to push my clouded heart forward, around the last switchback and up the hill John had mentioned earlier in the day—even if it did occur at a slug's pace. *Slow and steady wins the race*, I thought.

As soon as I got the idea for the campfire, I went outside and neatly stacked a pile of wood beside the circular rock fire pit behind my house, then ran upstairs and rummaged through my closet until I found my wedding album. There it was, stacked under three other photo albums. I slightly lifted the other albums and pulled it out, then sat down on the carpet and began to flip the pages. I perused each one slowly so I could appreciate one of the happiest moments in my life on paper one last time. It was a wonderful, bittersweet moment, admiring the whole album from beginning to end.

When I had finished looking, I closed the album, put it under my arm, and deliberately made my way downstairs. I grabbed some matches out of the antique buffet cabinet by the door on my way outside. I knew that part of my life was at an end and it was very important for me to move forward—sort of along the lines of the Tibetan healing mandala, where the monks create this elaborate sand design over several days out of millions of grains of colored sand, and at the end they sweep it up and plunge it into flowing water, which represents the impermanent nature of existence.

Outside, I sat the album on one of the wooden stump seats next to the fire pit, then walked to the woods to collect sticks and twigs for starter. I retrieved some newspaper out of the shed, crumpled it up in the pit, and added the wood, then went back inside the house to get two bottles of my favorite beer, Gaelic Ale, and a pack of almond M&M's I had been saving for an occasion like this one. After making my way back outside and sitting down on the stump beside the album, I put my treats down on either side of me and proceeded to light the fire.

When my fire was at the roaring point where I knew it would remain lit for a while, I opened my first beer and made a silent toast to my album: "Here's to sixteen amazing years. Thank you for the love, the tears, the laughter, and the understanding . . . and for knowing it is time to let go."

I picked up my wedding album and pulled the first photo out. The shot was of my dad and me in the church hallway, just before we walked down the aisle, and I was looking up at him with tears in my eyes but a smile on my face—exactly what I was feeling at that moment. I rubbed my finger over the photo for several minutes, contemplating putting it back in the album. I guess if someone was observing me from the outside, I might have looked a bit mad, but I was actually much calmer than I had thought I would be in this moment, on the verge of erasing this history of my life on paper.

The fire was full and there was no chance of saving a photo if it was placed anywhere close. With shaking hesitation in my arm, I finally placed the first photo in the fire and watched through a blur of tears as the flames sucked it in and it melted away into a multitude of blue, orange, red, and yellow hues.

16
Bag of Rocks

I am a great believer in variations on the routine.

—*Charms for the Easy Life*, by Kay Gibbons,
born May 5, 1960, Nash County, North Carolina

The next morning the sun was waking up in the east beautifully composed, ready to shine on the world, as I made my morning coffee. My soul, however, woke up humming a nocturne—specifically, Frederic Chopin's "Prelude in E-Minor (Op. 28 No. 4)."

Why was the paperwork—the finalization—gnawing at my spirit so intently? I thought I had bid farewell to my former self the night before, but now, as I hummed the same composition that was played at Chopin's funeral in 1849, I realized it was going to take more than a campfire and blowing grains of sand away for my heart to let go.

When I reached the parking lot where we had agreed to meet, Sam wasn't there waiting, but he pulled in shortly after me and parked horizontally, taking up three spaces---to give him space for a quick, clean get away, I supposed. The boys stepped out of Sam's car, and with somber faces and a slug's pace, made their way over to my car. The short ride to school, I kept hoping for words to come, but all three of us were at a loss for words. I managed to tell the boys I loved them when they were getting out of the car, but the slamming of their doors closed my words in.

The immense echo of that cold exchange stayed with me throughout the day and into the night. I crawled in under the silence of my covers early that evening, hoping sleep would help me escape, but at 1:00 a.m., exhausted from all my tossing and turning, I got up, made a cup of tea, and sat at my desk to write Charlie an e-mail.

From: Carrie
To: Charlie
Subject: Quiet House

Charlie,

I'm not sure if I told you today was the first day I exchanged the boys with Sam as officially divorced. I don't know why the exchange today was so poignant for me. This switching of the boys has been going on for a year now; funny how a piece of paper can bring tears to surface. This morning felt surreal, it was like I was watching a movie of what I've been doing for the past year replay over and over, but I was viewing it from the outside in slow motion . . . extra slow back up the mountain and throughout the day.

After I dropped off the boys at school I took my nervous energy and worked outside in the garden. I moved all the timbers to the backyard that I got to build the steps down to my garden shed. I worked on my twig fence, raked, and made a few more vegetable beds. I feel like I gave myself bicep tendonitis. I hope that's all it is. It must be from all the repetitive motions of cutting, drilling, hauling, and raking in one day.

Maybe you can come and give me some ideas on my steps tomorrow; I'm not that good at carpentry work. I iced my shoulder, so hopefully if we do any work I will be able to help.

I'm glad we have each other to listen to our bags of rocks. I hope I can carry as much weight for you someday.
Carrie

From: Charlie
To: Carrie
Subject: Quiet House

Carrie,

Stop beating yourself up. You've just been through a major life crisis. I think you have done a great job with Nelson and Quinn and you continue to do a nice job working through issues, no matter how difficult. It is a contest between you and your boys to see who has grown the most this year. I'm sure you all will emerge as winners.

Take care of yourself and if I can help with anything, let me know. I do want to help with the stairs and I have a few ideas. I will bring a carpenter's square to make sure your step timbers are at right angles and also a level to teach you a few things. Give me a call when you get up so we can arrange a time. We may be able to catch a short ride out of Fletcher after we work on the steps.

Hang in there, good friend and biking buddy,
Charlie

I was finally able to fall asleep after sending my e-mail to Charlie, and I slept late into the morning. When I woke, I turned over and stared out my balcony doors into the dense woods that surrounded my home. The wind was bending the branches and fluttering the leaves around like a merry-go-round. The dancing circles of the branches kept me hypnotized, and I laid there paralyzed, full of the double life I had been living. The boldest question swirling in my unsettled mind was the one I had no idea how to answer: *How and when will I reveal my true self?*

You're divorced now, Carrie. You're free to stop keeping the lie within and to live the way you want to live and love whomever you want to love. So the natural next step is just to come out to everyone, right?

My stomach lurched at the thought. I couldn't do it. I wasn't ready for my sons to know. For now, this "lie" was actually a survival tactic.

I finally managed to gather enough energy to roll out of bed and walk with heavy feet to the bathroom before going downstairs to the kitchen. I made oatmeal and coffee and sat down at my desk. My weary feelings made me queasy, so I was only able to eat a few bites of my oatmeal before I decided to call Charlie.

"Hello," I said, trying to sound cheerful. "Are you ready to come over and work on the chain gang with me?"

"What time would you like me to be there?" he answered without hesitation.

"As soon as you can get over here; I'm hoping to keep my mind on work and not family. My shoulder feels a lot better, so I think I can help rather than get in the way."

"I can get ready and be there in about an hour, say around eleven."

"Sounds good, just come around back when you get here. I'll be working in my garden."

"All right. See you in about an hour—and I'm bringing my bike so we can ride afterward. I think it would be good for you to get on your bike."

"Wonderful. Hopefully we won't use all our energy on the steps."

I wandered back upstairs to put on my work clothes and made my way outside to my garden. I no longer had to call it a "makeshift" garden; it was bountiful now, with raised beds separated by rich brown paths made from mulch. In the beds, an abundance of my favorite flowers—asters, chrysanthemums, lavender, cosmos, black-eyed-susans, purple cone flowers, zinnia, sunflowers, and Russian sage—brimmed throughout. The flowers encircled my vegetable beds, and I now grew enough food to share with friends at dinner parties on my back porch. Nelson and I had made a metal arbor from rebar at the entrance with a prolific climbing pink and deep maroon clematis vine that welcomed new growth each spring. My garden was where I escaped to be with the silence of the wind and let my weaknesses blow away for a bit; it was the place where I put all the love that I had no idea how to give Sam or Ryann. I had loved them both fervently, but in the wrong place and at the wrong time. Each love had been transitional and important, which would last a lifetime in my dreams.

I put on my rubber garden gloves and started mixing the compost, soil, and peat into my new beds. *Where will my journey take me next?* My feelings were outrunning my thoughts that morning, and I was having a hard time figuring out how to tame them. Luckily, there was always digging. I set myself to weeding and working on my new beds, and lost track of time for a while.

I was reaching for my hoe when Charlie came around the corner.

"Hello," he said, smiling big. "I can see you're already busy working away."

"Yep," I said, smiling back. "Just thought I would get in a little warm-up before the steps."

"Shall we get started on them?"

"I'm ready," I said.

I led Charlie past the lavender and around the clematis arbor to the top of the hill, where the timbers were piled high for my steps. I had a circular saw, ruler, and extension cords lying beside the pile.

"What next?" I inquired, as I pointed to everything on the ground with both hands. I thought I knew exactly what to do next, and I was sure he suspected I was about to make a big mess.

Charlie looked down at me through his glasses and smiled. "Let me go get my level and carpenter's square."

He disappeared around the house and I stayed there to admire my prized timber, which I'd salvaged from some workmen who'd put water lines up on the mountain in the fall. Charlie had helped me trudge through the muck and stack the timbers in the back of my truck. We'd both been covered in mud by the time we unloaded them at the house.

I smiled to myself as I remembered him promising the summer before that he was going to ignore me when I brought the word "job" up again as we fumbled together putting screens on all my doors. Or the time when he helped me apply poison to my admirably tall hemlock trees to kill the woolly adelgid beetle that was attacking them. I ran from under one of the trees, arms flailing as I was pulling at my hair while screaming "Spider!" at the top of my lungs. I'd even talked him into putting lights on the outside of my house once, without much assistance from me. He said I was like Huck Finn: that my jobs always seemed to grow into bigger jobs, and then into great adventurous jobs. But here he was once again, lending me a helping hand.

Charlie came back with his tools in hand, and we went over to the hill to measure the area for the steps. That done, we began to cut the timbers and drill holes through the thick posts. Charlie sawed the initial set, so I could watch and learn, and then I did some of them.

As we dug out the first opening in the slope for the timbers, I turned and squinted up at my friend. "Thanks, Charlie."

"For what?"

"For helping me do this and not thinking that I shouldn't because I'm a girl. A lot of people would have blown me off and encouraged me to hire someone to do it."

"I've never doubted you or your ability to do anything you want to do. I think you're going to scare yourself when you realize your own potential."

"Blah blah blah, potential. *Inconsequential* is what I feel. If I have so much potential, then why am I divorced, brokenhearted, and all alone?" I said, sighing. "Though just to set the record straight," I added hastily, "I'm not feeling sorry for myself."

"Just as I said, you have not realized your potential. And it does sound like you're feeling sorry for yourself," Charlie said sternly. "All of those things you just mentioned are a part of life—especially if we choose to experience all of it, including the good with the bad."

I was looking at Charlie intently and not paying attention to what I was doing.

"Whoa, slow down," he said. "You're beating the lumber with your worry."

"Oops," I said. I looked down and realized I'd been stomping harder and harder on the timbers as we talked.

Charlie patted the front timber with the handle of the shovel. "Now it's beyond time to check with the level," he said, handing the tool to me. "Take it and see what we need to do to make this one right. You may have to add some dirt back under this side."

I knelt down and laid the level on the lumber. "I don't know, I just feel like I should be making a difference in the world in some way, and I don't really think I'm doing it. How naive does that sound, 'make a difference'? Isn't that what we're supposed to focus on in our twenties? I feel like I'm coming of age in my forties."

He giggled a little. "Yes, you are; this is an important time for you. You have been home with the boys and taking care of your family, so now is the time to build your career and focus on developing you. And don't forget you've already made a difference in the world with your two boys."

The level was off in the front, so I pushed some loose dirt underneath the wood to bring it back up. "I guess, but I feel like I'm floating in the wind."

I managed to level and square the first step. I smiled a proud smile as I looked up at Charlie for approval. "Can we hammer the rebar in now?"

He looked down and nodded. "We can take turns pounding in the rebar; it will probably be the hardest part."

I jumped up and grabbed the sledgehammer. "Okay. I want to go first."

The first two dings of metal-to-metal contact were easy, but the louder and denser the ding sounded, the more strength it was taking, and my muscles were not quite strong enough to finish the job. I kept hitting the rebar, but it seemed to be stuck there. I finally took a break when I missed and scraped my hand enough to bring blood to the surface.

"Ouch." I stood up and rolled my shoulders forward with exhaustion as I let out a heavy sigh, but kept a tight grip on the hammer. I didn't want to give up.

I looked at Charlie and he already had his hand palm side up, reaching out for the hammer with a smile on his face.

I accepted defeat and handed him the hammer. "Charlie, are there times in life when you wake up in the morning and you wonder how you ended up here? Because that's what I felt like this morning. I've wondered and keep wondering how I got here and where am I going next."

"Of course, life is full of those times, and wondering about how you got here is good. Just so long as you don't get lost in your curiosity and have a hard time finding your way out. I still think it would be good for you to go to the support group that meets at All Souls."

"Nah . . . I'm more of a one-on-one whiner—never liked the idea of sitting in a circle and talking about my issues or problems to strangers. I can always start counseling again, but I really felt like I needed a break from it."

"Okay. I won't bug you again about the support group; just keep it in mind for when you're ready." He bent down and swung the hammer at the protruding rebar, and it disappeared into the wood instantly.

We spent a few more hours out in the hot sun laying timber and constructing steps up the steep incline. The work was hard, and it felt good to move toward the top of the hill; it felt like a mirror for what I was trying to do with my life. As Charlie and I dug, sawed, hammered, and sweated together, I thought of my life and tried to visualize an understanding of my new identity and how it would fit into the lives of the people I loved.

17
A New Life

I'm a tar heel through and through.

—Unknown

The boys settled into a routine and became comfortable with living between homes. I missed them awfully but began to fill the empty spaces with learning the ins and outs of my new career. It was hard to get a job as a forty-two-year-old recent graduate who had been home for sixteen years taking care of two boys, but after graduation I successfully passed my boards and secured a job in a skilled nursing facility doing rehabilitation with a wide range of patients. The most challenging ones—those with dementia of many different types—soon became my most beloved patients.

I celebrated my forty-second birthday as a career girl and left my stay-at-home life behind.

From: Carrie
To: Charlie
Subject: New job

Charlie,

I had the most wonderful birthday ever. The day started out with a huge card hanging on my office door. It was covered in barely legible scribbles from my patients and signatures from my favorite staff. The speech therapist somehow made a copy of a picture of my darling patient, Gabi, as a small child in her Bavarian opera costume along with her dad and brother and placed it at the bottom of the card. The best card you can imagine . . . I'm really happy to be working now outside of my home.

They gave me a decadent chocolate ice cream cake for lunch. Gabi sang "Happy Birthday" to me five times throughout the day because it was new to her each time that it was my birthday. She still has a beautiful alto voice. She also told me over and over again, with an amazing smile on her face, that I wouldn't be working on my birthday in Germany. She would add, with her fingers to her lips, "Germany has so much more finesse—all the beer and wine you can imagine on your birthday."

I came home, and Nelson drove Quinn and me to dinner at Tupelo Honey across from Gerber Village. Nelson and Quinn were really sweet and let me talk about my day the whole dinner. Nelson gave me a gift of three coffee mugs, and Quinn made an extra-special card with a tree he called Carrie's Tree. Under the tree is the caption "It's a new year. Conquer the world."

We made our way home to another surprise: Myra and Brenda were waiting with another cake and round of "Happy Birthday." Oh, and my voice mail exceeded its capacity with so many "happy birthdays"; I'll be forever returning thank-you notes. I am just so completely blessed with so much at this moment in my life.

Carrie

From: *Charlie*
To: *Carrie*
Subject: *New job*

Carrie,

I am really happy you had a great day. I still don't think you understand what a wonderful person you are. You attract and keep great friends, because you are such a good friend to everyone.

Do you remember how anxious and frustrated you were two years ago with your career and having chosen to stay home with your boys? Now, after all the anxiety, you may have found your true calling and joy in working with old people.

You look more relaxed and happy than I've seen you in a long time. Just think how far you have come in the last six months. It is amazing to me. I'm sure there are more interesting things in store for you in life.
Charlie

My interview for my new job was quite the experience. The facility was north of town, tucked into the side of a mountain in a place where it was hard for the sun to peek in, and as I drove up the dark approach, it became evident that it was an old, washed-out elementary school that had been converted into a nursing home.

When I arrived, I punched in the combination I'd been given and entered the front door, only to be hit with the scent of stale urine. I would soon learn that housekeepers in nursing homes can work over time and still fail to overcome that smell; it always seems to be drifting in the background.

I went to the window and tapped on the glass that separated the office clerk from the front hallway. She looked up with a slight scowl on her face, as if I had interrupted something very important, and ever so slowly slid the glass to the side to communicate with me.

"Hey," I said. "I'm here for an interview with the therapy department."

"You can have a seat on the couch over there," she said, pointing across the hall, "and I'll let them know you're here."

I barely had a chance to cross my legs on the cold vinyl before a scruffy dog with the short, stocky body of a Corgi started sniffing my ankles. He worked his way up my leg but decided that wasn't close enough, so he jumped up on the couch and scooted right up next to me. I shoved him with my left shoulder a little—after all, there was a whole other end with no one on it—but this backfired on me: instead of running him off, it excited him. He rounded his back, wrapped his forefeet around my shoulder, and started humping me vigorously with his whole body. In the process of his vigorous behavior he tangled his feet up in my hair. Embarrassed and uncomfortable, I reached over and gave the dog a thrust—but did it a little harder than I intended. The dog fell completely off the couch and hit the tile floor with a loud thud.

Crap! I covered my mouth with both hands and squeaked in a gulp of air, then looked up and down the hall to see if anyone had noticed my awful mistake. All I saw in close proximity were a few residents who looked like they had no clue about where they were in time and space.

Once the dog had regained his composure, he trotted away down the hall with an aura of confidence. I could have sworn he had a smile on his face.

Within seconds my interviewer was hovering over me. "I see you met Jake the resident dog."

I reached up to try and straighten out the mess Jake had made of my hair. "Oh, does he live here all the time?"

He reached his hand out to me. "John, pleased to meet you—and yes, he lives here all the time."

I shook his hand firmly. "Carrie, pleased to meet you also."

He gestured down the hall. "Would you like to go on a tour first?"
"Sure."

As John showed me around, he was very personable with the patients, and introduced me to a few as we passed by. We made a quick loop around the building and back to the green couch.

"Have a seat and I'll be right back. I need to get some paperwork."

My nerves were shot. I hoped Jake would not reappear again. *Is John really going to interview me here for the whole world to see?* I wondered. As I waited, two visitors passed by and knocked on the window of the front desk, and the receptionist took her time opening the window, showing them the same unhappy frown she'd shown me.

John came back and sat in a chair beside the couch, and launched into a barrage of typical first-time interview questions. I got through the first two questions without any mishaps, but just as I was about to answer his third query—"Tell me your greatest strengths first and then your weaknesses"—he looked over my shoulder and intently said, "Stop."

I was afraid to look back, so I stumbled a little through my answers. "Oh . . . this is the time you want me to brag. I'm not a very good bragger, though. . . . I guess you could say that's my greatest weakness: not knowing when to toot my own horn."

He looked up from his pad with a slightly puzzled look. "All right, so what would be your greatest strength?"

I hesitated with my answer, because the baffled look he gave me made me think I was answering the questions all wrong. "Um . . . well, let me see . . . I'm very empathetic and a good listener, and I feel that's an important attribute in this setting."

He asked another question, but before I could answer, he looked over my shoulder once more and said, "Stop!"

This was totally confusing me. *Is he speaking to me or to someone behind me?* I didn't want to look back over my shoulder to find out, worried that it would seem rude.

John followed up the next two questions in the same manner, with a "Stop!" to the air over my shoulder, but now each time he said it he was also moving his hand in the air like he was swatting a fly away. This made me wonder if he had Tourette's or some other syndrome I had never heard of. I was still afraid to look over my shoulder, I thought I might offend him.

Finally, John seemed to notice my confusion, because he looked at me with wide eyes and said, in a voice just a bit louder than a whisper, "I'll explain when we're done."

I made it through the rest of the questions with just a few fretful stumbling episodes over my words, and there was a short, awkward pause as he flipped through his papers and studied them for a bit. Just when I thought he was finished, he asked one last question to close the interview: "Is there anything else you would like to add?"

My heart began to race, because I was at a loss for words. I shifted myself on the couch to buy a little bit of more pondering time. I was already convinced I had bombed the interview and there was no way I was getting the job. Then my younger sister, Jody, appeared in my mind, and I blurted out without thinking, "My little sister calls me 'the old people whisperer.'"

John looked at me with surprise on his face. "Really?"

"Yep, she's called me that ever since I adopted an older couple in our neighborhood when we were growing up. I mowed their lawn, chauffeured them to and from the grocery store, and just spent time with them. They were an amazing influence on who I am today."

"Old people whisperer . . . I've never heard that before." John looked as though he was contemplating what I had said as we stood up and shook hands once more.

We walked side by side to the front door, and before I walked out, he pointed behind us. There was a haggard-looking double amputee sitting in the hall, his hand resting on Jake. John punched in the combination to get out, leaned over toward me, and whispered, "He was giving me the middle finger all through your interview."

"Oh . . . goodness," I said, looking up at him with disbelief in my eyes. It was the only thing I could think of to fill the void. "Well, thanks for the opportunity to interview."

"You're welcome," he said. "I'll be in touch real soon."

My mind was full of questions on the way to the car. I wasn't sure if I was ready to work in a lockdown facility with low-level dementia and Alzheimer's patients—but then again, I was pretty sure I wasn't going to get the job anyway. I was even more convinced of this when I looked in my rearview mirror before backing up only to discover a large clump of hair sticking straight out on the left side of my head. I quickly pushed it down. "Boy, I really obliterated that one—and no thanks to you, Jake!" I said to myself out loud.

I stopped to get groceries before going home. I was twisted up with hope and fear, and made my way up and down the rows tossing things in the cart without paying much attention to what I was putting in. I was pushing the cart out to my car when my phone rang.

"Hello?"

"It's John."

I gulped. "Hey. How are you?"

"Good. We would like to offer you the job."

I didn't even hesitate. My heart was racing with accomplishment; I couldn't believe the speed at which my life was changing. "I'll take it," I said gleefully. "When do I start?"

"Two weeks . . . and I want you to know, it was the "old people whisperer" thing that scored for you."

I started my new job two weeks later, as promised, and when I found out that my very first patient's name was Charlie, I knew I was where I was supposed to be.

18
Sopaipillas

I think the main reason my marriages failed is that I always loved too well but never wisely.

—Ava Gardner, born December 24, 1922, Smithfield, North Carolina

Two years had passed since our divorce was final, and Sam still got eerily nervous around me. He could barely look at me, and always walked away without speaking whenever we had to meet. I kept my sadness hidden behind a fictitious courage when I was around him. I felt it was the least I could do; I still felt an overwhelming sense of blame and responsibility for the breakup of our family.

One Saturday, the boys were supposed to spend the weekend with Sam, but just as I thought they'd left, I heard the familiar sound of two doors closing, followed by the equally familiar sound of car tires screeching around the switchbacks heading back down the mountain. Seconds later both boys came inside, shoulders slumped forward, frowns on their faces.

"What's wrong?" I asked.

"Dad got mad at us because he said we were talking back to him, so he brought us home," they said in unison.

I needed to dump my bag of rocks somewhere; naturally, I did it in an e-mail to Charlie.

From: Carrie
To: Charlie
Subject: Sam

Charlie,

Sam became angry with the boys again and brought them home. I think that's three times in the last couple of months. Now he will disappear for at least a week without contact. The boys never hold it against him. I try every day to tell Nelson and Quinn how they have no responsibility for the wrong reactions Sam and I make as adults. I do know how important their relationship is with Sam and that whether or not it is the best, it is irreplaceable. I have a difficult time filling his shoes when he disappears. I guess I could be bitter about our situation, but I think both boys have great opportunities, and to be bitter would be a waste of time. It could be a lot worse or a lot better—depending on which "Joneses" you're looking at. We can always compare, but who do we compare to and in which way?

Thanks for being a positive male influence in their lives. Quinn really enjoys golf and the after school math help you give him. Nelson went to Flat Rock Playhouse with his class today and saw *Tuesdays with Morrie.* Are you familiar with this book? It reminds me a bit of our story. Nelson said he had tears welling up in his eyes. I hope it is true and I have raised sensitive boys to become sensitive men.

I know this is last-minute, but can you and Anne come over for dinner Saturday? I went out to my garden and picked the last of my summer basil tonight and made some fresh pesto. I can freeze it, but it would really be better fresh. Let me know, it is the least I can do to repay you for all your help.
Carrie

PS: One of my favorite quotes from *Tuesdays with Morrie* is "Forgive yourself before you die. Then forgive others." I wonder if I forgive myself if it would help Sam forgive me??

From: Charlie
To: Carrie
Subject: *Sam*

Carrie,

If you can teach your boys to be sensitive, they will be such a success. It is the greatest gift you can give them. I think it is important that they realize that their father's difficulty with this divorce is not their fault. They also need to realize that they will have to deal with difficult teachers, friends, bosses, and maybe spouses all their lives, and yet they can learn from all of them.

I enjoy playing golf with Quinn and the math helps keep my mind young. You have struggled with a number of challenges for so long. Just sit back and take the help. Speaking of help, it is coming close to estimated tax time. The ride Saturday is Terry's Gap/Little River. Do you want to stop at Earth Fare after, get a cup of coffee, and work on them together?

It seems to me that up till now you have had some very strong-minded men in your life making your decisions for you. In addition, your boys kept you busy enough not to have any free time. For the first time in your life you have time alone to think about who you are and what you are doing. It is a new process for you. I think you really have a wonderful person to get to know better (I mean you). Oh and let's not fail to mention a divorce, aging parents, coming out, and a new job. I think it is time for forgiveness.

Yes, Anne and I will make dinner and pesto sounds great. The food is so good at your house; it is just like going out to dinner for us. Let us know what time to be there.

Take care,
Charlie

After telling me what happened with their dad, both boys stomped up the five stairs and to the end of the hall. Their room doors shut almost simultaneously with a burst of emotions behind their slams. I stood at the kitchen sink, looking out at the multitude of soft mountains unfolding in the distance, and thought about how my life was full of emotional mountains. For every peak of change I managed to climb up, another one was waiting on me. I was trying to understand this new territory that was lying in front of me—that this was the very nature of existence: you're guaranteed change.

I couldn't come to terms with how Sam felt it was acceptable to take his anger and turn it on the boys. To understand his anger was easy, but how he could hurt our boys in the process was incomprehensible to me. I knew there were times when he loved our boys more than life itself. They were his favorite pastime; the minute he walked in the front door his smiles were centered on them. I still remembered all those nights after dinner when he'd spent the entire rest of the evening in the family room on the hard wood floors tickling, wrestling, and pillow fighting with them, even though he had hours of charts to dictate back at the office. And I knew Sam would have been there until the end. I was the one who hadn't been able to do that. Because if I'd stayed I would have woken each morning with a low, humming voice inside reminding me that I was trying to be someone I really wasn't . . . and I'm sure it would have found a way to echo into my nights.

My sons were still trying to comprehend how their single world had become double. It wasn't an easy thing for them to understand—they were so young—but at times I thought they were carrying the weight of the world on their shoulders. They worked hard at appearing to be strong on the outside while they kept their hurting feelings inside, not realizing they couldn't hide those feelings from me. Moms have this extra-strong antenna for their children's pain, without the privilege of an off switch. I could tell that as time was passing they were gradually adjusting, and beginning to smile a bit more. But when things like this happened—Sam taking his anger at me out on them—it was like they took ten steps back.

I turned away from the window and leaned the small of my back into the sink, my heart heavy with guilt at the thought that I was partly the cause of the turmoil my boys were going through at the moment. I knew I had to wipe the disgrace off my face soon and go upstairs to try to soothe their hearts. I stood there frustrated, my arms dangling down by my side, for a few minutes longer before I took a few deep, agonizing breaths in and ventured up the steps.

Once I was in front of the boys' doors, I paused with a long sigh and looked back down the steps, contemplating whether or not I should make a run for it. After all, I was much better at running away from my troubles than facing them head-on.

I squeezed my fists tight and shook them in the air out of frustration before I knocked lightly then laid my hand flat on Quinn's and then Nelson's door, hoping to feel or hear a reply.

Quinn's door slowly pulled away from my hand first, and he began to scrutinize me with his little blue eyes through his thick glasses. In a bleak tone, he growled out, "What, Mom?" It sounded more like he was saying "go away" than like he was actually questioning why I was there.

"Would you like to talk?" I asked, worry in my voice.

"No." He started to close his door again, but I stopped it with my foot. Nelson was rustling around just a bit in his room; it sounded like he was trying to hide his noise behind the door. I knocked once more, and he finally opened the door. Now they were both looking at me with hurt frowns. I felt a deep hole of sadness open up inside me. A slide show of how we had been as a "normal family" crawled through my brain, extra slow, as I stared at my boys, and I tried to think of the impossible: how to cheer them up. I knew I couldn't, because I wasn't their dad.

Their faces were red and blotchy from crying. "Would you like me to make some sopaipillas?" I asked. Their favorite food was the only thing I thought might have a slight chance of raising their spirits.

"Yes," Quinn answered first, and Nelson followed quickly behind with, "Yeah." Then they both tried to close their doors at the same time.

I pushed my hands firm against their doors a few seconds longer. "I'm here any time you want to talk," I said, knowing they wouldn't want to—they never did when their dad brought them home. Their doors closed, and out of the corner of my eyes I could see my hands quivering. I was so afraid Sam had already told them what I so desperately needed to tell them myself. I felt a restless urge to knock on their doors and expose myself right in that moment, but the feeling disappeared as quickly as it had appeared.

Empty and afraid, I ran downstairs to seek refuge in my kitchen. Cooking was just as therapeutic for me as biking and gardening were. I could disappear in the act of preparing the food and hope it would bring some type of organization to my confusion.

In the kitchen, I leaned my forehead against the cupboard doors and stared at the flour, imagining a day when my boys would understand my "different love." After a few dazed minutes, I began the long process of mixing, kneading, and waiting patiently on the sopaipillas to rise. The first part is the blending of the sugar, yeast, and warm water. As I gave the ingredients a chance to do their dance from the bottom of the bowl up the edges, my mind twisted between the space of my anxious thoughts and the evolution of the soft pastries.

Once the mixture became bubbly, I whisked in the right amount of flour to create a sponge pliable enough to knead. This was my favorite part of the process. While pushing, pulling, and then reuniting the dough, I envisioned myself squeezing the hate Sam harbored for me right out of him, hoping he could find it in his heart to forgive me.

As I set the dough in the oven to let it rise, my phone rang, and Jackie's number lit up on the front. A couple of years had passed since we'd gone on that first ride together in Asheville, and her last words on that ride—"I think I said, *everyone* involved"—were still ringing in my ears.

As I reached for the phone, I knocked the flour off the counter with my elbow and it fanned out across the room.

"Hello?" I said, flustered.

"Hi," Jackie said. "What are you doing?"

I leaned back into the sink to marvel at the chaos I had created around me. "I'm making a big mess, along with dinner for the boys."

"What's for dinner?"

"Sopaipillas—they're these little fried pillows of bread that I usually fill with refried beans, then I save some to stuff with jelly and sprinkle powdered sugar on for dessert."

"Sounds yummy! But the real reason I'm calling is to see if you have thought about the trip to Italy any more?"

Of course I had thought about it; we spoke about it at least every other bike ride. Jackie had been nudging me for the past year to travel with her somewhere completely new for a bike trip. It was to be my forgiveness trip—a journey of exploration into whom I had become, a trip during which all my guilt was supposed to be left behind.

With a long sigh into the phone, I thought about how I had barely been out of the eastern United States, much less across an ocean. It also startled me to think of experiencing life so far outside of my box of daughter, wife, and mother. Jackie and I had scanned travel catalogs for hours together, and I kept planning on doing the trip in my mind, but for some reason I couldn't bring myself to sign on the dotted line.

"Yes, I think about it all the time," I said to her now, "but I'm still having a hard time being selfish."

"Carrie, it's not selfish. You need to let go of your hesitation and experience life on your terms."

"I'm trying, I really am."

"Well you better try harder, because the deadline for the deposit is Monday."

"I know. Let me think about it," I pleaded, "and I promise I will get back to you by the end of the day."

"Okay," she said. "I plan on hearing from you—and it better not be tomorrow!"

We hung up, and I commenced to rolling out the sopaipillas. I thought of all the extra hours I had worked to save money for this trip. How could I let it slip through my hands? With my first cut into the soft dough, I decided I was going to go to Italy—but I knew I needed to make a real commitment or I would back out again. So while the triangles were rising the second time around, I called the tour company and made my reservations for the trip. *In just a few short months, I will be pedaling along beautiful, rolling vistas past sunflowers and poppies*, I thought, and for the first time in hours, I smiled.

———

The boys and I barely spoke during our meal. Their faces had cleared up, but they still looked sad enough to be sulking over a lost pet, and they continued to avoid discussion of their short trip down the mountain and back. Meanwhile, I was stuck inside my head, feeling their hurt and entertaining thoughts of a forgiven life.

19
Italy

Claim your space. Draw a circle of light around it. Push back against the dark. Don't just survive. Celebrate.

—Charles Frazier, born November 4, 1950, Asheville, North Carolina

I was eastbound for Italy at the same time Quinn was traveling south to Honduras. My destination seemed overly decadent when contrasting it with Quinn's trip: at age forty-four, I was planning to spend my traveling time being selfish with my appetite, body, and soul amid breathtaking beauty, while my sixteen-year-old son was going to a third-world country to help the people there with health care, education, water safety, and dental hygiene. My friends kept reassuring me that both trips were important at these stages of our lives. I was going to learn about forgiveness and letting go of guilt, while Quinn was to learn about giving and letting go of selfishness. My trip to Italy would overlap Quinn's trip to Honduras by three days, so I was depending on Charlie to welcome him home.

From: Carrie
To: Charlie
Subject: we made it

charlie,
     i'm on a public computer at antica fattoria la parrina and i
have no idea how to find the shift key. some of the keys are funny

little symbols i've never seen before. i'm having a wonderful time.
we jumped off some tall rocky cliffs into the mediterranean sea . . .
boy, was that water cold and salty. afterward they had a picnic
with so much food and a 360 degree view of the sea circling us.
tonight we are in orvieto on an estate where they produce and
grow all their own food, including their animals to eat, olive oil,
cheese, balsamic vinegar, flowers, vegetables, and the best part . . .
vino. there's a cornell graduate student doing her veterinarian
internship here.

tomorrow we will be riding our bikes to an olive oil farm.
the countryside here is charming and exquisite with sunflowers
around every turn. it's hot and we get started late so the heat
is very intense. i'm eating so much and i'm really feeling it on
the hill climbs. i might not ever come home . . . hope all is well
back in asheville.

i received an e-mail from gail, who is in charge of the hon-
duras trip. i will forward it to you. they are waiting on a rsvp
for the welcome-home party. i was hoping you could go in my
place, since i won't be home in time.
carrie

ps: i'm attaching quinn's e-mail to me on what he is doing in
honduras . . . quite a contrast.

To: Mom
From: Quinn
Subject: Honduras

Mom,
    It's Quinn. I'm in Santa Lucia. We went to the schools on
Friday and we will be visiting them all this week. The kids are
a big hit, they're very nice and excited to see the gringos—ha
ha. We are visiting a lot of markets around the little town. The

markets are small and have limited food, but it's cheap, and pretty good. The roads aren't gravel or paved; the best way I think you can imagine the roads is to picture a river without water, seriously!

The school that I'm visiting, San Francisco, is small, with 173 kids in K–6. They run around with each other and kick small plastic soccer balls during recess. That's about it for physical education. Soccer is their favorite game. The teaching is much different here, it's challenging for the teachers to discipline the children, for instance trying to keep them in school without leaving and going outside to do whatever. I understand that it's difficult for the teachers, especially when you have the guy who is in charge of the school (I suppose the principal) running back and forth teaching the 5th and 6th grade.

The kids like to play soccer with me and they like to listen to my iPod. I let them listen to songs. This coming Thursday we are having a good-bye party at the schools, so we'll give them a few gifts. Then Friday morning we're leaving to La Ceiba, I guess that is how you spell it, where we will be staying for a week with our translators, who are a big hit with us. Their English is fantastic because they began when they were three!

Hope you're having fun in Italy,
Quinn

From: *Charlie*
To: *Carrie*
Subject: *we made it*

Carrie,

You can be sure that you're missed. Neat pictures. I see you are not too tired for wine and you have already figured out that black is worn everywhere in Europe. You're not in West Virginia anymore.

I hope you are having a very special time. For everything you have gone through in the last four years you deserve every moment without guilt. Have some fun and don't worry about anything.

Thank you for taking the extra time to send me some pictures. It is nice to see you in a completely different situation. Your amazement with life is just beginning.

Charlie

PS: I was going to send an e-mail to Gail introducing myself and letting her know I will be the one at the welcome home party. I will be the backup for everything. Enjoy!

From the moment we landed in Rome, I felt how alive and vibrant Italy was. I first witnessed it while standing in the baggage claim area, where I watched locals interacting in ways I had never seen before: they combined their arms, fingers, and mouths in movements that looked like a choreographed dance piece.

Our first destination was Orvieto, a small city north of Rome. The drive should have taken close to an hour and a half, but our driver was Italian, so it only took us an hour. My eyes were huge around each curve and my heart skipped beats throughout the ride. Everyone around me was calm, as if we weren't flying through the air like a torpedo, so I gulped my panicked shrieks to the back of my throat and sequestered them deep down.

Orvieto was built on a volcanic plug of tuff rock, so it looked like an eruption of ancient buildings sprouting from the earth. We stayed at Hotel Duomo, which was right around the corner from a legendary Gothic cathedral that towered completely over the small town. It had been there for three centuries, a fact that made me ponder the infancy of America—how we are a mere newborn in Italy's eyes.

Shortly after we arrived, Jackie and I walked the streets for hours to explore the shops, which carried locally made goods of all sorts. The streets were vibrant, alive with people. Every hour, church bells with distinctly different chimes echoed off the narrow streets of the city just seconds apart. The cars were extra small, like the Smart cars back home, and there were scooters around every corner, weaving in and out of traffic. The brick and cobblestone roads, as well as the ancient buildings, were a baked rust color resembling the clay-packed bridle trails I rode my bike on growing up.

We got lost in the city until just after dusk, when the air cooled and the sunbaked streets and buildings began to radiate a clean smell. Before leaving a wine shop, I turned to the older gentleman behind the register and, raising my hands high above my head and shaking them, asked, "How do we get to the cathedral . . . uh, Duomo?" I was learning to use my arms and hands in conversation as they did. I pronounced it again, this time really slowly, because I was sure I had said it wrong: "Du-o-mo?"

He smiled, as if laughing a little at my accent, then swung his arms around and pointed upward, out the window. With a thick Italian accent, he said, "You follow roads up; always up will lead you back to the Duomo."

I nodded with a smile. *"Grazie."*

He threw his head back slightly and let out a friendly chuckle. *"Salire* . . . go up."

Getting sidetracked in the streets of Orvieto was inevitable, but after a few roundabout circles we managed to weave our way back up the narrow roads to the main square, where we found a quaint café below the shadow of the cathedral. We sat under a yellow umbrella enclosed by bay trees and ordered food. By the end of the week I would be feasting on things like *crostini di fegato* (liver pâté crostini), *arista alla fiorentina* (Florentine roast pork), *cacciucco* (fish stew), wild boar (one of my favorites), truffles, and lots of *pecorino toscano* (sheep cheese), but at this point in the trip I was still afraid to branch out of my American box, so I decided to stay safe with my order: I asked for fresh pasta and orvieto classico white wine.

When the waitress brought us our wine, Jackie held up her glass.

"Cheers. Here's to Italy and our first glass of Italian wine. Now, let's celebrate new beginnings and leave divorces behind."

Courage rose up inside me. "Here, here. I'll second that." Then, feeling a bit flustered, I slowly leaned back into the chair and sighed out, "Speaking of new beginnings and affairs . . . Jackie, I have a new beginning to talk to you about."

She frowned a little bit as she sat her wineglass down. "What do you mean?"

"I mean I have more than my divorce and starting over without Sam in my life as a new beginning. It goes much deeper than that. I'm hoping you will understand and *forgive*, as we have spoken about." My knees were shaking together under the table and I chanted to myself, *Remember, slowly but surely wins the race. You can reveal yourself to one friend at a time . . . when you are ready. The last time I checked, nobody had the book on coming out mastered.*

"What could be more than your divorce and starting over?" she asked, looking confused.

"I don't know any other way to say this . . . but . . . Jackie, I'm gay." Just like that I blurted it out, and although it scared me to do it, a huge wave of relief hit me the second I said it. I didn't have to make the effort to hide who I was anymore . . . I could just be.

Jackie held her glass high once again and answered almost instantly, with reassurance and sternness in her voice this time: "There is no other way to say it, Carrie, and why should there be? Thank you for trusting me to understand."

It was as though she already knew, but she had given me the respect and time to let her know when I was ready. I nodded at her with appreciation and said what I had heard on the streets all day— "*Grazie, grazie* . . . my friend."

She said "*grazie*" right back, and we sipped our wine. And that was it—we didn't speak about it over the meal or for the rest of the trip. I was really quite relieved about that, because I wasn't yet ready to go any deeper than telling her I was gay.

When the waitress came over with our food and I took my first bite, I grinned. "I think this is the yummiest thing I have ever put in my mouth."

"I told you this would be a trip of a lifetime and you would enjoy every minute of it, especially the scenery and the food," Jackie said, smiling back.

"Oh Jackie, this is beyond anything I could have ever imagined or done. I'm awestruck at the history surrounding us and the pasta and the wine . . . what words can describe this moment? I feel like I'm in a fairy tale land. Thanks for encouraging me to come."

"I'm glad you came."

We stayed in our green corner until well after the chimes rang nine and then walked under the moonlight on the cobblestone road back to the hotel. Once in the room, I opened the windows and settled my arms on the sills, and there was a woman who looked to be a grand-mother on her flower-filled balcony just below and across from me. I felt like I could almost reach out and touch her. She looked up and saw me, smiled, and waved. I inhaled the warm, dark air and waved back.

I lingered at the window for at least thirty minutes more before going to bed. Jackie was already sound asleep, trying to wear off the jet lag that was holding on to our bodies. It seemed to take forever, but I finally fell asleep as well. The last thing I felt before succumbing to sleep was an overwhelming sense of happiness.

—

I woke early to the sputtering sounds of scooters moving about out-side and rolled over.

"Jackie, are you up?"

She turned to me and pried her eyes open. "Yes . . . why?"

"I was just wondering. I'm extra excited about this trip."

"I'm glad," she said.

"I want to thank you again for persuading me to come and for being such a wonderful support system."

"I'm your friend," she answered quickly. "And that's what friends do . . . spend time together and support one another."

I chuckled under my breath. "In exotic places like this?"

"Yes, Carrie, they do."

"I guess you're right. This is just a first for me."

"You've probably needed to do it for a long time. We can get caught up in taking care of everyone else and forget we are neglecting ourselves."

I rolled off the side of the bed and jumped up. "Well, thanks again anyway. It's eight thirty—do you think we should go get some breakfast since we have to be back at the van by ten thirty?"

Jackie nodded. "Yes, I think we should."

———

We left our luggage in the front lobby and walked down into the center of town to a little café with a terraced dining area outside, where we had cappuccinos and fresh croissants with jams and Nutella. I had never tried the hazelnut and cocoa spread before, but as soon as I did, I was hooked.

We stayed on the terrace, watching passersby, until just before the church chimes struck ten in the distance, then walked briskly back to our van. When we got there, our guides, Nicholas and Aryanna, were already loading our bags.

Two hours later, we arrived at an estate dating back to 1200. The deep-green vine creeping all over the outside of the white stucco mansion resembled the strawberry vines back home in my garden. We gathered under an awning just outside the small hotel and listened to instructions from Aryanna.

"Everyone should go to the desk just inside the doors," she said, pointing to a green door to our right. "They will give you the keys to your rooms. Once you've checked in, come back out here to the event center to the left and we will have lunch before orientation."

Jackie and I were put in the charming Gigliola room, which had two single beds and antique furniture covered in vibrant floral prints. We quickly got dressed in our bike attire and ran back downstairs to the event center where a feast from the surrounding estate farm waited for us. After eating we were left to wander and explore the roads. We rode for hours in the July heat, past rows of grapevines, olive trees, flowers, and vegetables. That evening, as every other evening for the rest of the trip, I had no trouble falling asleep.

—

Early the next morning we rode our bikes to Talamone, a town on the western coast. The motorists along the way seemed to be comfortable with and respectful of cyclists, and they made wide passes around us. Once in Talamone, we put our bathing suits on and headed for a popular ridge to go swimming in the Mediterranean. At the top of the rocky, sand-colored ridge overlooking the sea, I stood in silence for a moment, mouth gaping, and took in the beauty. In the distance, on the cliff opposite us, was a famous villa called Torre Saracena.

"Oh my, Jackie, look at that water, it is such a pretty blue. It's like none I've seen before."

"Let's go!" she said, and ran down the oleander-lined steps full of translucent pink petals, as I trailed her ankles all the way down toward the water.

In the distance was a platform jutting out from the rocks that provided easy access for diving into the sea. We put our things down at the bottom of the stairs and ran to the platform. The sun shimmered on top of the crystalline sea, making it look as if thousands of broken mirrors were floating on the ripples.

"Wait, Jackie—let's jump on the count of three together," I said, feeling giddy.

"Okay," she agreed eagerly.

"One . . . two . . . three!" I shouted, and we leaped into the cold, salty water.

I hit the rocky bottom and bounced right back to the surface to see Jackie already treading water and peering over at me.

"That was so much fun," I said, grinning. "It felt like being a kid again. It's been a really long time, Jackie."

"You're right, it was fun," she said. "What better way is there to act but like a kid? Play all day, fill your belly with food, and go to bed late and exhausted."

I smiled at Jackie in agreement, and she turned to swim out deeper into the water, her tiny body moving seemingly without effort over the ripples. I followed quickly behind her, and when we'd put a little distance between us and the platform, we both turned on our backs to enjoy the warm sun on our faces.

I let a few moments pass before I turned back toward Jackie. "I want to remember this moment forever, Jackie—to keep it safe and bring it out when I need a reminder."

"A reminder of what?"

"That there can be beauty after great pain—you just have to let it show its face. That's what I want to keep reminding myself."

———

Our week in Italy included a visit to the beautiful Giglio Island, where lovely, bronzed bodies in itty-bitty bathing suits and sometimes no tops at all sunned themselves on the beach. We also rode under long tunnels of pine groves and learned the labor-intensive art of harvesting pine nuts. Every summer I had pondered where pine nuts came from as I was gathering basil to make pesto for dinner parties. Now I understood why Italian pine nuts were so expensive.

We visited an olive oil farm and learned how the family members— from two-year-olds all the way to seventy-year-olds and beyond— participated in the entire process, whether that meant climbing the trees, pressing the olives, or packaging the product. We also learned how to detect fresh oil versus rancid oil, and I knew from that point on I would be an olive oil snob.

In Orbetello I had my first Italian gelato. After struggling with all the choices, I was finally able to narrow it down to three flavors: *nocciola* (hazelnut), *cocco* (coconut), and *cioccolato fondente* (dark chocolate). I got the largest size possible, and after that day I was unable to pass by a *gelateria* without begging, "Let's stop and get some more, please . . . please!"

We spent the last day of our bike trip exploring the busy, romantic streets of Rome and ended the evening at a small pizzeria where I had my first slice of *true* Italian pizza. I stuck with the basic—*pomodoro* and *formaggio*, which is essentially cheese and tomatoes—but on that day the cheese and tomatoes took on a whole new flavor. It made me sing inside with each bite, Luciano Pavarotti–style, *All'alba vincerò!*— "At daybreak I shall win!"

As the opera *Turandot* goes, like the prince who thought he would eventually win the princess's hand in marriage, I knew I would conquer my fears of being gay and come out a winner. The grand finale of that day was washing it all down with the house vino from the Sabine Hills, just outside Rome. . . . Happiness.

20
Blue Apples

I am a real rebel with a cause.

—Nina Simone, born February 21, 1933, Tryon, North Carolina

Ayear after coming back from Italy, I decided to run a tour of my own—in West Virginia, appropriately. I invited ten of my closest friends along. It was time to reveal to them who I really was. I was desperate to let go of all the fear I had piled up inside; I had become an expert at swallowing it back down, but I didn't want to do that anymore.

The majority of the tour would run north on seventy-eight miles of old railroad bed that paralleled the beautiful Greenbrier River. I hoped to be done with feeling guilt over being true to myself by the end of the trip.

Charlie had back surgery a few months before the tour, so he wouldn't be able to join us for the ride, but in his typical, generous fashion, he helped me with planning and carrying out the logistics.

From: Carrie
To: Charlie
Subject: Tour

Charlie,

I'm sorry your back was not healed all the way and you were unable to ride on the tour. Your help with sagging, grocery

shopping, and cooking the chicken on the grill was so appreciated.
I don't think I could have pulled it off without help from you.

Believe it or not, I was an ugly duckling growing up. Pudgy
little tomboy and almost never fit in anywhere I went. I feel like
I've always had to work hard to achieve, but now it is paying off.
It was safer to stay in the closet but not truthful, so I decided to
go for it. I was so worried the night I told everyone. If I tell my
story, I hope it gives other people the courage to be themselves
and live life on their own terms.

Thanks for your support through every step of the way. Now
I just have to tell my boys . . . whew!
Carrie

From: *Charlie*
To: *Carrie*
Subject: *Tour*

Carrie,

Even though I was very sad I did not get to ride a bike, the
trip to West Virginia was wonderful. Everyone had a great
time and the planning of the activities was terrific. And your
own style of leadership worked to bring the group together. The
B&B in Marlinton was great and the house in Cass was perfect.
We are all good friends and got to know each other so much
better sharing a house and hearing your story.

After this trip, I began to realize how far you have come
from the timid, worried, self-depreciating person that I knew
when we first met. You are now self-confident enough to come
out to your friends and let the world know who you really are.

You are now willing to take risks to realize your dreams. It's
wonderful to see you grow so much. I kind of miss the clingy
person that I could supposedly inspire or maybe you were just
being nice.

However, the powerful Carrie is terrific to know and now I am the one who is learning about life thanks to you.

In the interest of my blood pressure, please do not jump out of the airplane until you have checked your parachute, even if your job really is not your dream job. You will make a terrific bike tour leader if you choose to make that your career.

Seeing you finally achieve independence from your own fears and move forward is kind of like watching a daughter go out into the world; immensely fulfilling, but also creating anxiety about the challenges you will face. As I have said many times, my advice is worth every penny you pay for it and it comes with a lifetime guarantee.

Charlie

The Greenbrier River Trail is one of the best examples of the hidden paradise West Virginia has to offer. I may not have grown up in those majestic mountains, but West Virginia is deep in my blood—so deep that it leaves me breathless every time I pass through East River Mountain Tunnel and cross the state line. After all, it was my first home away from home, and I also gave birth to my first son, Nelson, in those coal-rich Appalachian hills.

We began our ride at 8:30 a.m. on September 8, six days before my forty-fifth birthday. Our route would take us from the southern terminus in Caldwell through Greenbrier County, then into Pocahontas County, and finally to the northern terminus at Cass. I could have just as easily organized an awe-inspiring road bike tour through Greenbrier County, West Virginia, or back home would have been even easier, but there was a very important reason I arranged my tour along a railroad bed traveling north: I had promised myself I would disclose my own underground secret by my forty-fifth birthday once we reached the remote railroad town of Cass.

The secluded gravel trail we followed on our ride runs just above the Greenbrier River, passing through valleys and deep woods, and alongside rocky cliffs, all along the way. The first steam locomotive traveled south across the railroad bed on October 26, 1900, carrying virgin lumber extracted from Cheat Mountain to its final destination, the West Virginia Pulp and Paper Company in Covington, Virginia.

When Sam was in medical school, I put in mile upon mile pedaling along that trail; some days, hours passed without my ever encountering another person. Each season in the area also offered something distinctly precious that was visible only because the river was untamed and civilization had just slightly touched the trail. Spring was the time to witness nature's wildflowers—trillium, jack-in-the-pulpit, columbine, Jacobs's ladder, and goat's beard—blooming. Summer was when it was hot enough that the hens were laying hard-boiled eggs and it was time to drink from the honeysuckle vine and use one of the rope swings along the way to jump into the cool Greenbrier River. In the fall, the trees let go of their leaves, which twirled downward, leaving candescent bits of red, yellow, and orange speckled carpet upon the remote gravel path. And winter provided the best opportunities for cross-country skiing and the wonderful peace of hearing snow fall and listening to your breath move in concert with it. In every season, mornings became my favorite time to ride, because that was the time of day when I was most likely to see the misty fog holding itself over the river like a ghost dancing with the water.

On one occasion, I was lost in the hum of the trail passing by, when a huge black bear lunged onto the path about twenty feet in front of me. I abruptly skidded my bike to a stop and remembered what I was taught by the old-timers in town: remain calm and slowly move backward, away from the bear. I tried my best to hide my fear while, still straddling my bike, I began my cautious retreat. It took a moment, but once the bear realized I was there, it turned in the opposite direction and barreled, quick as the wind, back up the mountain. Chills went from my head to my toes as I stood there trembling. I listened for a few moments to the heavy rustling of the leaves as the bear disappeared into the distance, and then I jumped on my pedals and rode away as fast as I could. After a few miles, when I was almost totally out of breath, I finally calmed down enough to realize that the bear was probably just as scared of me as I was of it.

Today, as I rode with my friends, I squeezed the horn Charlie had given me before we left at each mile marker. I was probably being quite obnoxious, but I was marking something important: with every mile we completed, we were creeping closer and closer to my having to expose the secret I was holding within.

The spookiest part of the tour, but also one of the most thrilling, was going through Droop Mountain and Sharps Tunnel. From 1899 to 1900, Italian immigrant stonemasons carved through the sides of two separate mountains—a distance of more than nine hundred feet total—to create a path from one side to the other. The tunnels were sooty, wet, and rocky, with water dripping from the arched rooftop, and in the middle we were surrounded by humid black air, making it hard to see light at either end. The tunnels are not for anyone who is claustrophobic or scared of creatures that may loom in the dark. The saturated anxiety of my mind felt like it was on the verge of collapse. With each pedal stroke through the thick, musty blackness, I felt the Droop Mountain tunnel pressing heavily down on me—but at the same time I felt relief knowing there was a stay overnight in Marlinton before I had to divulge my secret.

I couldn't say the same for the Sharps Tunnel the next day. Now there were only thirteen miles to the finish, and the wet drops from the rocks above hitting my arms were a cold reminder that time was closing in on me.

———

In Clover Lick there was a remodeled depot that used to be a water stop for the trains; this was our rest area on the second day. After that we rode the last nine miles to Cass, where we stepped back in time to a town built at the turn of the century around the railroad and lumber industry. There was a little hump of a hill right before town that we couldn't see over until our bicycles peaked at the top—the kind of hill that throws your stomach into a downward loop, like an elevator dropping too fast, when you reach its crest and start to descend. I felt that thrill and my mind jumped, reminded that there was no turning back now; tonight was the night when the walls I had built around myself would forever be withdrawn. I blew out a loud *whew*, but no one heard because I was tooting my horn at the same time. We had reached our final destination.

Once we got over the hill, there were rows of white-boarded homes with white picket fences and boardwalks in front of them as far as we could see. These were the company homes for the loggers, now turned into vacation homes. Very little had changed in Cass since those logging days except there were no longer stacked piles of maple, cherry, birch, spruce, oak, and hemlock sitting by the railroad tracks, ready to be loaded on flat railcars. Now tourists were going in and out of the company store, which served as a restaurant and gift shop. The steam engines still filled the air with their noise, but only traveled north, carrying tourists to Whittaker Station, Bald Knob, or the abandoned town of Spruce, high up in the mountains, at 3,853 feet.

We arrived at our company house on the first row, just a few yards away from the Greenbrier River, and after a quick lunch, we caught one of the trains headed to Whittaker Station. The railway had to be designed with two switchbacks up the mountain to be able to climb the steep grade. As we chugged past the rusted skeletons of equipment and buildings, left over from the defunct lumber business, I thought about the task set before me. Tonight was the night.

—

After the trip back down the mountain, it was time for dinner and a revelation I wasn't so sure I was ready to divulge to my friends. Kara, my neighbor, had graciously come along to assist Charlie with sagging—picking up people who'd gotten tired, making needed repairs, and so on—and, in her words, be the "hired help." As the three of us were in the kitchen, preparing dinner, I was dancing around, kicking my legs every which way in an attempt to get rid of the nervous, jittering jerks I was experiencing inside.

"I can't do it," I whispered to Kara. "I just know I can't. What will they think?"

She had started out being supportive, but now she worked her way toward sternness with me. "Probably what I thought when you told me more than a year ago: I had pretty much figured it out already. You were never dating men, and all I ever saw you bringing around were girls."

I let out a short, snickering chuckle before saying, "Well, it did help that you were easy to talk to."

"Exactly. These are your friends, and I believe they will understand. You'll be just fine."

I did a little wiggle, held my spoon up in the air, and twirled it around in the steam escaping from the boiling noodles in front of me. "Maybe not, I might lose one or two of them. What if I lose all of them?"

Kara stopped working on the bread she was buttering and looked at me with a funny smile. "Carrie, you're not going to lose them. Don't worry about it."

"How would you know?" I answered, sounding like a smart-aleck teenager. "You're not the one who's been hiding for so long."

"Stop it," she said firmly. "I don't want to hear any more about it, and you will tell them at dinner as planned."

I closed my mouth and finished up cooking while she set the table.

"That was fast," I said, as Kara walked back into the kitchen empty-handed. I was hoping for more stall time. "Isn't there more to prepare in there?"

She pinched her lips tight together and gave me a strict look. "No, it's all done, and it looks as though you have everything else ready in here. It's time to take the food in."

"All right." I didn't say anything more.

My heart was frozen and trembling as we carried the food to the table. I was absolutely wound up inside about delivering my news. Charlie was the only other one in the group who knew my plans.

All ten of us sat down at the extra-long table to eat. A blackberry cobbler was baking in the kitchen, and it sent a sweet aroma floating through the house. I tried to block out the real world and looked at each of my friends, imagining what their reactions would be when I told them. I envisioned one or two being uncomfortable with who I really was, but for the most part I assumed they would accept the new me. I stayed in my sheltered dream world while I watched everyone enjoy one another's company until all the food was gone and it was time to speak the truth.

Under the table, my sweaty, shaking hands were crumpling the paper I had written many years earlier. I had carried it with me with each move I'd made, hoping that I would eventually find the courage to reveal its true intent one day. Now I was rubbing it so intensely that I could feel little pieces of paper landing on my legs. It was no use; my nerves were out of control. *I'm not going to tell them*, I decided—but no sooner had I made my decision than Charlie spoke up beside me: "Carrie, don't you have something to say to all your friends here at the table?"

My mind went blank and I couldn't find any words. Tears almost surfaced. I was really lost; I didn't know how to come back.

Kara, seeing that I was nervous, joined Charlie: "Yeah, Carrie, let's hear it—what are you waiting for?"

Ooh-wee, I was hurting inside. It was a strong hurt that had been lurking for years—one I didn't know if I could conquer at the moment. I looked from one end of the table to the other, barely making eye contact with anyone. Then I did a long peer at Kara in front of me and to the left at Charlie once again, assuming they would save me—like, maybe throw me a lifeline and reel me in. But no. Neither one of them was planning on bailing me out.

Charlie could tell I was about to back out. He gave me a little poke in the side. "Carrie, you're among friends and we will all support you. Go ahead, let everyone know."

I slowly pulled my hands up to the top of the table, along with the crinkled-up paper, and reluctantly began unfolding it. I looked up from it and paused a moment as I contemplated putting it back under the table, but again I got the look from Kara and Charlie, so I pushed forward.

"Guys, I have something to tell you about me that may come as a complete surprise. Do you mind if I read this and then explain?"

A few answered "yes" out loud, while others shook their heads in agreement without speaking words. Some had puzzled looks upon their faces.

The writing on the paper was barely legible, after all the contorted movements I had done with it while I had it hidden under the table. I still didn't have the courage to unfurl my secret place on my own, so I prepared myself in my mind and I began reading with my best friend's accent from first grade. She was African American, and we never got to hang out beyond school, but I loved that girl just like a sister. Every day I woke up excited and ready to go to school because I knew I was going to get to spend the day with her. I did my best to channel her voice as I read:

> My daddy once told me, "Long about Virginia way, you can see blue apples along the Underground Railroad. They're blue with stardust from the night air." He said, "Rumor has it, at this stopping place, if your timing is right, the light from the moon shines a glitter on the apples with a luster of sapphire."
>
> Oftentimes I've dreamed about those blue apples. When I feel the hot sun burning my back and the dust from the dirt seems to rise up to my knees. When my hands are stinging so from picking the white man's gold . . . I dream of those blue apples. When I see my pappy or a friend being whipped, I imagine myself under a tree full of blue apples. When I see sweat running down the overseer's cheek or his horse's thighs as he stares while he moves from row to row like a mean snake . . . I dream of those blue apples.
>
> I will vanish from this place someday so I can see and hold those blue apples. I no longer want to see my father's, brother's, or sister's hearts swollen with sorrow. I'm going to run from here, pick one of those blue apples, and cradle it in my arms, knowing I'm on my journey to freedom. The pain this place

brings to me I can no longer bear. My legs, my arms, and my feet want to run as fast as the wind and never look back. I feel the freedom blood running through me like a wave; I know it will come to pass soon.

I was born Chaquela Graham in Creswell, North Carolina, on a wheat and rice plantation. I got my last name from my master. My mammy and pappy were only allowed to give me my first name. All slaves take the last names of their master in these parts. . . .

I slowly peered up from my paper to see everyone staring at me with wrinkled-up noses and bewildered looks upon their faces. I'm sure they were wondering, *What does this have to do with you?* I turned my eyes back down to my artifact from the past and gently folded the wrinkled paper. My mind was running in circles, trying to conjure up words to explain what I had just read. I drew in a few long breaths and sighed out extra slow, hoping the breaths would help me organize my thoughts.

"I wrote this over fifteen years ago, when I came to terms with the fact I was gay," I said, my voice shaky. "I decided the right thing to do was to keep my family together. I told myself the only way I could leave was through my mind, so I did it vicariously, by writing a book about a slave who escapes all the way to Canada on the Underground Railroad. The only thing is, I never came to terms with Canada being far enough away—so I stopped writing that story and started writing my own instead." My voice was getting stronger now. "I know it is not anywhere near as perilous as running on bare feet in the dark of the night while looking over your shoulder, all the while hoping not to hear dogs barking or horse hooves stomping along somewhere in the woods. But it's been quite scary for me; even telling all of you the truth tonight made my heart seriously think about having a heart attack. And there you have it . . . all of you know my story now."

I barely took a breath between what seemed like one nervous run-on sentence, because I so awkwardly wanted to get it all out. I looked out of new eyes at the friends surrounding me and, clasping my hands over my paper, I sighed out before breathing in deep once again. My heart still felt etched with little chills; I had told my friends now, but where would I find the courage to tell my boys? I imagined that was going to be much more difficult. I knew the hairs on my arms would stand up when I approached them with my truth.

———

After everyone had gone to bed, I tiptoed out onto the front porch and stood quiet with my eyes closed for a moment, savoring the fall air. It seemed as though I was the only one in Cass awake except the night insects humming all around me.

I looked out over the top of the picket fence to the river. It was bright enough outside that there was no need for a front porch light. I stood and studied the flecks of moonlight waltzing with the ripples upon the river, then made my way over to the porch swing. I pumped my legs and listened to the soothing sound of the Greenbrier River flowing past as I tried to organize my thoughts. I imagined the river traveling south—over river rocks, around switchbacks, all the way past Marlinton, Denmar, and Renick and finally reaching Caldwell, just below Lewisburg, where my journey had begun more than twenty years before. *I suppose this is how life travels,* I thought. *Over, under, and around many switchbacks.* My travels started when pain and fear were larger than hope and desire for me, so . . . I married Sam and began calling West Virginia home.

Under the radiant moon that night, I looked down at my arms and imagined that I was holding the bluest apple in the world tight against my chest. I started crying—soft tears, so no one could hear, but inside I was singing a powerful hallelujah chorus. These were thankful tears: I had shared my truth, and all my friends were still my friends.

I stayed on that swing, cradling my knees, and inhaled love and exhaled love until the sun chased the moon down behind the mountains.

21
Courage

The harder it hurts, the louder it bleeds.

—Me, born September 1966 and raised in the
Piedmont of North Carolina

I pined over the inevitable for another year before finding the courage to tell my boys about all my years of *hiding*. Where would I
start . . . back in sixth grade, when I first experienced the "in love"
fuzzy feeling for girls instead of boys? Or when I was nineteen, hearing the eerily quiet voices of virtue singing in my head, "It's wrong;
you have to like men"? There were many days when they would be
asking me questions and I would be oblivious to their repeated pleas
of "*Mo-om*." Instead I was in another world replaying my deceit in my
mind and trying to come up with an easy way out. I wanted them to
know that lying to myself didn't mean my love for them was not true.
How would I make them believe they had not been part of a lifelong
lie?

As each year went by, I had fallen deeper and deeper into a facade
that I had created because I thought it was the right way to be. The last
thing I wanted to do was cause my boys any more pain or hurt. But
for all their lives, I had preached to them about always speaking the
truth—I had told them that doing so was the only way to live. So now
it was my turn to practice what I had been preaching, but not living,
for so long.

From: Carrie
To: Charlie
Subject: Dinner conversation

Charlie,

Sometimes it's nice to be a child for the reinforced security, but we all have to grow up eventually. Quinn seems to be growing up quick; he's getting pretty serious with his new girlfriend. I had dinner with him and Nelson at Tupelo Honey tonight. We had some pretty open conversations, but not about the subject of being gay. Quinn did say vaginas are ugly and asked, "Can girls have more than one orgasm?" Nelson threw in his two cents or two words every now and then. I think he may have been a little shocked himself at the subject of the conversation. When we got home, Quinn blurted out, "I think I'm scarred, Mom." I said, "You're scarred? You brought the sex subject up—I think I'm scarred." He also informed me that his girlfriend, Jennifer, and her mom went to Planned Parenthood.

Well now you know how part of my night went . . . sexual conversation over dinner? I'm not planning on discussing my sexual preference with them for a while, but I'm happy they are not afraid to approach any subject with me.

Hope you were able to get work done around your house. I spent the day hiking the mountain and cleaning up my garden.
Carrie

From: Charlie
To: Carrie
Subject: Dinner conversation

Carrie,

Oh my! That is probably TMI for you. However, Jennifer and her mother going to Planned Parenthood is really scary. Hope it's for future prevention, not pregnancy?

It seems that Quinn continues his tradition of not being able
to find things; let's hope it's not condoms this time.
Charlie

One Saturday evening, I had a few friends over for dinner, and our conversation over appetizers turned from innocent to the sore subject of "When are you going to tell your boys?" I got a little defensive when the topic came up; I believed it was up to me and no one else to choose the perfect time to tell my boys that I had a secret I had been keeping practically my whole life. I also had a little wine onboard, which probably gave me the extra push I needed at that moment.

"I'm going to," I said, harshness in my voice. "I know none of you believe me, but I am. It's just really difficult for me to get both of them together—after all, Quinn is in college six hours away. What if I tell one and then he calls the other? It is hard enough to have a serious conversation with a twenty-one-year-old and an eighteen-year-old."

My friends looked at me with what I thought were eyes of judgment, and instead of hearing what they were saying, I lost myself in a daze of worry. In my mind I was replaying what so many friends who were not in the room had said to me in the past: *You should have already done it by now. I think your boys already know anyway.*

My button pushed, I pulled my phone from my pocket, thinking, *Fine, I'll tell them right now.*

"Hey, guys," I wrote. "Sorry to approach this way . . . in texting . . . but I want you to know I'm gay . . . Hope you will still consider me your special mom . . . 'cause I know I was born to be your mom."

The first text I got back was from Nelson: "I've known for a long time now. I don't care, you're my mom and I'm proud to have you as my mom . . . no worries."

What a relief. Now the waiting began for Quinn to answer.

Finally, after what seemed like forever, he answered as well: "I'm gay too . . . gay for the pussy."

What could I say to that? I decided to try to make light humor of the situation, because I didn't know what else to do. So I texted Quinn back what came to my mind first: "Well, God bless us both."

He texted me back, "Good one, Mom. Ha ha."

Well, he answered back with "Mom," so that's a good sign, I thought—but it really wasn't my goal to turn the situation into a joking matter. The phone went silent for another really long pause. When I decided I couldn't stand the dead air anymore, I called Nelson.

He answered on the third ring. "Hello?"

My nerves caused me to take in a few silent gulps, but I was only able to stand the sound of my heart beating in my throat for a few seconds. "Hey . . . I'm sorry I texted that to you . . . I know it wasn't very appropriate. I just hit my breaking point and I wasn't sure when Quinn would be home from college again. You two never seem to be in the same room with me anymore, unless it's Christmas or Thanksgiving."

"It's okay, Mom, I promise."

"Are you sure?"

"I've known for about three years. We were just letting you tell us in your own time. It was a bit of a hunch, but Dad had been telling us he was sure of it for a while and we just put two and two together. We're both happy for you."

That's what everyone had been telling me: that my boys knew. I just kept negating it in my mind, too afraid of this moment of disclosure to really hear it. I was so scared I would lose my boys—that they would close the door on me forever if they knew.

"Is Quinn mad at me?"

"No, Mom, he is just a little shocked; he knew too, but was just staying in denial because it was easier."

"I know, believe me I know . . . seems like I've been living in denial forever. Well, I will try to text him again because he quit answering, which is making me a little nervous. Thanks for your support. I love you."

"We love you, Mom . . . just the way you are."

As soon as I hung up I texted Quinn again, "I love you. I may not be the best at my tact as a mother, but I always mean to be."

A few more anxious moments passed slowly by with me staring at my phone's blank screen and rubbing my extra-sweaty palms together.

Finally, the phone lit up and this came through: "You are too the best . . . Love you, Mommy."

I was still having a difficult time letting go of my guilty feelings, so I texted again: "Just don't think badly of me."

"Love you forever and ever and I don't care."

Static doubt was tugging at my heart. I guess too many years of trying to live up to the perfect Southern lady was bubbling over. "Really . . . well I just couldn't be a loser and hide anymore. Thank you for forgiving me."

Finally, I ended my high-speed wobble with victory in my heart and my arms high above my handlebars, embracing the world on my own terms. Just before I turned out my light that night, one last text came through from Quinn—the best thing you could end a day or a lifetime with: "Proud of you, Mom . . . I love you."

Epilogue
January 2015

From: Carrie
To: Charlie
Subject: Thank you

Charlie,

I hit the breaking point and texted my boys tonight. No more hiding—they know now. Nelson and I spoke on the phone right away and he is very happy. Quinn initially said, "I'm gay too . . . gay for the pussy . . . Mom." I thought I taught him more respect than that. Then he proceeded to call Nelson right away and say, "How random is that, Mom is gay?"

Is it 100 or 1,000,000 thank-yous? It should be the latter, but I'm not sure if that is even enough! You have helped me with so many things I couldn't imagine trying to conquer on my own. Thank you for cheering me on all along the way.

Carrie

From: Charlie
To: Carrie
Subject: Thank you

Carrie,

I am so proud of you. You can finally have a completely open and honest relationship with your boys. At least Quinn still called you "Mom." He is an emotional guy inside and probably needs some time to process it all. My bet is it won't be too long.

This is such a big step for you. I am sure this will lead to wonderful things. No worries about thank-yous—sounds like you are stressing too much over the small stuff.

Sleep well, angel to so many. Someday you will look back on this and say, "Gee, I had to put up with a lot of shit."
Charlie

My boys accepted me and my lifestyle so easily, it makes me wonder why I hid for so long—why I let fear stand in my way. We have always had a strong relationship, but the bond has become much stronger now that I don't have a deep-seated secret gnawing at my soul anymore. Our connection with each other is finally surrounded with serenity and trust.

Ryann has since left her husband and now is married to a woman. I found a rich and wonderful life up on my mountain in North Carolina, and she has found joy on her mountain in West Virginia. We made our peace with one another mostly by being thankful that our stories collided when they did, and that we helped one another get to where we needed to be—living real and loving honestly.

I can't say the same for Sam. I think I hurt him too much. When we were together, he was as patient and loving as could be expected with the mysterious pushing-and-pulling energy I threw at him each and every day. I'm sorry that there is still an awkwardness between us that causes us to avoid each other at all costs. But I'm not sorry that I loved him and created a family with him. I am most grateful for our two boys. Tomorrow cannot change what happened, but my hope is that it will somehow bring forgiveness and healing between us.

Asheville has always been known to be a pocket in the South where acceptance is more prevalent, so I'm happy to call it home—to live somewhere where I'm able to feel comfortable with who I have become. When I travel elsewhere in the South, I usually don't speak of being gay. I guess some would say it is my own homophobia peeking out, but I'm not convinced of that. It is something you can experience only if you live in the South day in and day out, like the certain way a person turns their head, the way they stare or point their finger. It is what you experience only when you have Southern family members or friends who don't agree with your lifestyle choices—which is usually because of stereotypes they have been taught.

Change seems to move a little more slowly into the South, but I believe that as time passes, fear will realize that love is love and it's extraordinarily simple to understand. "Gay" love will be thought of as being just as natural as loving a spring morning stroll through a blossoming garden or staring up at the twinkling stars on a clear night . . . or it will become one with "straight" love. There will be no need for anyone to question it, and no need for bravery to show it. No more pointing fingers, no more staring, and no more fear or hate crimes to kill what is misunderstood. One of these days, everyone will just feel it, and they will know that it is love.

In spite of the challenges I've faced as a gay woman in the South, I never left the mountains. I think it's because I enjoy the climbs and the switchbacks so much. The slow pace on the ascents, the quick downhills, and the mystery that lies around the sharp curves—ever changing. I've learned a lot through the switchbacks life has to offer, and the most important rule of all is this: ride the paths slowly, and enjoy every moment—whatever riddles the next turn may bring.

Acknowledgments

Writing a book is absolutely not a lone effort. It has team work written all over it, and I want it to be known that I had an amazing group of people on my team from beginning to end.

I am deeply grateful to all who stood by and encouraged me along the long road of writing, editing and rewriting my manuscript. I'm especially grateful to my immediate family Austin, Seth, Kate, Cathy, James, Jane, Jody and Nena. My Aunt Maryann and Uncle Rojdah for the extra love and understanding. All of you gave me perfect support and feedback as I made you listen to my drafts over and over through the years. Thanks to my adopted family, Janet, Judy, Jeff, Susie, Edie, Gerry, Sue, Art, and Jane for believing in me. Thank you Hattie for telling me it is more important to try than it is to succeed.

Thanks to Brooke Warner of She Writes Press for taking a chance on my messy manuscript and sending me to the wonderful editor, Annie Tucker, who, with sensitivity and patience, helped me turn it completely around. I'm also indebted to copy editors and project managers Lauren Wise, Krissa Lagos, Pamela Long, and anyone else who worked behind the scenes to get my manuscript worthy of printing.

Thanks to all my friends who came to West Virginia on my bike trip and loved me unconditionally. As I said in one of my emails, thank you Pat for letting me borrow Charlie.

This could go on as a whole chapter, so for those I have not mentioned please forgive me, and thank you for being in my life. Thank you for the love and memories.

About the Author

© Jane Coates

*C*arrie Highley grew up in the piedmont of North Carolina before moving to the mountains and completing her bachelor's degree in Therapeutic Recreation at Western Carolina University in Cullowhee, N.C. After moving up and down the east coast for fifteen years she has settled down in Asheville, N.C. She is an active member of Asheville Writers of Asheville, Blue Ridge Bicycle Club and Adventure Cycling Association. *Blue Apple Switchback* is her first book.

SELECTED TITLES FROM SHE WRITES PRESS

She Writes Press is an independent publishing company
founded to serve women writers everywhere.
Visit us at www.shewritespress.com.

Uncovered: How I Left Hassidic Life and Finally Came Home by Leah Lax
$16.95, 978-1-63152-995-5
Drawn in their offers of refuge from her troubled family and promises of eternal love, Leah Lax becomes a Hassidic Jew—but ultimately, as a forty-something woman, comes to reject everything she has lived for three decades in order to be who she truly is.

Loveyoubye: Holding Fast, Letting Go, And Then There's The Dog by Rossandra White $16.95, 978-1-938314-50-6
A soul-searching memoir detailing the painful, but ultimately liberating, disintegration of a twenty-five-year marriage.

Fire Season: A Memoir by Hollye Dexter
$16.95, 978-1-63152-974-0
After she loses everything in a fire, Hollye Dexter's life spirals downward and she begins to unravel—but when she finds herself at the brink of losing her husband, she is forced to dig within herself for the strength to keep her family together.

Insatiable: A Memoir of Love Addiction by Shary Hauer
$16.95, 978-1-63152-982-5
An intimate and illuminating account of corporate executive—and secret love addict—Shary Hauer's migration from destructive to healthy love.

Breathe: A Memoir of Motherhood, Grief, and Family Conflict by Kelly Kittel
$16.95, 978-1-938314-78-0
A mother's heartbreaking account of losing two sons in the span of nine months—and learning, despite all the obstacles in her way, to find joy in life again.

Renewable: One Woman's Search for Simplicity, Faithfulness, and Hope by Eileen Flanagan $16.95, 978-1-63152-968-9
At age forty-nine, Eileen Flanagan had an aching feeling that she wasn't living up to her youthful ideals or potential, so she started trying to change the world—and in doing so, she found the courage to change her life.